MW01079098

# Liberty

## DON TROIANI'S PAINTINGS OF THE REVOLUTIONARY WAR

# DON TROIANI'S PAINTINGS OF THE REVOLUTIONARY WAR

Art by **DON TROIANI**

Text by **MATTHEW SKIC**

Foreword by **PHILIP C. MEAD**

### CONTRIBUTORS

Lawrence E. Babits, Joel R. Bohy, David J. Jackowe, James L. Kochan, Bob McDonald, Eric Schnitzer, Robert A. Selig, Gregory Theberge, and Anthony Wayne Tommell

## STACKPOLE BOOKS

Guilford, Connecticut

Published by Stackpole Books
An imprint of Globe Peqout, the trade division of The Rowman & Littlefield Publishing Group, Inc.
4501 Forbes Blvd., Ste. 200
Lanham, MD 20706
www.StackpoleBooks.com

Distributed by NATIONAL BOOK NETWORK

To find out more about the artwork of Don Troiani, visit www.dontroiani.com.

Follow "Don Troiani Historical Artist" on Facebook.

For free information about the artwork and limited edition prints of Don Troiani, contact:

W. Britain
20 E. Water Street
Chillicothe, OH 45601
(740) 702-1803
www.wbritain.com

For information on licensing images in this book, visit Bridgeman Images, www.bridgemanimages.com.

Title graphic design by Rebecca B. Phipps

British Library Cataloguing in Publication Information available

**Library of Congress Cataloging-in-Publication Data**

Names: Skic, Matthew, author. | Mead, Philip C., writer of foreword. | Troiani, Don. Paintings. Selections. | Museum of the American Revolution, organizer, host institution.
Title: Liberty : Don Troiani's paintings of the Revolutionary War / art by Don Troiani ; text by Matthew Skic ; foreword by Philip C. Mead, PhD ; contributors, Lawrence E. Babits, Joel R. Bohy, David J. Jackowe, James L. Kochan, Bob McDonald, Eric Schnitzer, Robert A. Selig, Gregory Theberge, and Anthony Wayne Tommell.
Other titles: Liberty (Stackpole Books (Firm))
Description: Guilford, Connecticut : Stackpole Books, [2021] | Includes bibliographical references and index. | Summary: "A catalog for the exhibit of Troiani's work at the Museum of the American Revolution, highlights pivotal events of America's fight for independence. For the first time in a museum, this special exhibition brings together Troiani's original Revolutionary War paintings and pairs them with artifacts from the museum and private collections"— Provided by publisher.
Identifiers: LCCN 2021011765 (print) | LCCN 2021011766 (ebook) | ISBN 9780811770408 (hardback) | ISBN 9780811770682 (epub)
Subjects: LCSH: Troiani, Don—Exhibitions. | United States—History–Revolution, 1775–1783—Art and the revolution—Exhibitions.
Classification: LCC ND237.T637 A4 2021 (print) | LCC ND237.T637 (ebook) | DDC 759.13—dc23
LC record available at https://lccn.loc.gov/2021011765
LC ebook record available at https://lccn.loc.gov/2021011766

∞™ The paper used in this publication meets the minimum requirements of American National Standard for Information Sciences—Permanence of Paper for Printed Library Materials, ANSI/NISO Z39.48-1992.

Printed in China

*To my beautiful and patient wife, Donna,*
*who endured all my boring history stuff for decades.*

This book was published to accompany the special exhibition
*Liberty: Don Troiani's Paintings of the Revolutionary War*
at the Museum of the American Revolution in Philadelphia, Pennsylvania,
from October 16, 2021 to September 5, 2022.

Presented by

Education Sponsor

With additional support from

Pritzker Military Foundation on behalf
of Pritzker Military Museum & Library

Lanny and Ann Patten

NJM Insurance Group

 With appreciation for support from the National Park Service,
Washington-Rochambeau Revolutionary Route National Historic Trail,
for a new commission by Don Troiani, *Brave Men as Ever Fought*.

*This page represents all support pledged by April 1, 2021.*

# CONTENTS

# PREFACE

The American Revolution is my favorite period to study. It is fitting that this book should be published as the 250th anniversaries of the key events of the Revolution begin to be commemorated, with 2025 on the horizon. My collection of Revolutionary-era buttons, canteens, muskets, and cartridge boxes and my travels to battlefields and historic sites always remind me of the people who forged this nation. Those artifacts and stories inspire my work. It is my hope that my paintings help people today grasp the significance of the Revolutionary struggles of the people who lived 250 years ago, whose brave actions continue to shape our lives.

I cannot think of a better institution than the Museum of the American Revolution in Philadelphia to partner with to publicly display, for the first time, my original paintings of the Revolutionary War. This museum is a must-visit institution that presents dynamic, personal stories through films, immersive experiences, and exhibits of rare artifacts. I am particularly grateful for the support of R. Scott Stephenson (President and CEO), Philip C. Mead (Chief Historian and Curator), and Matthew Skic (Curator of Exhibitions).

Special thanks, as well, to contributing authors Lawrence E. Babits, Joel R. Bohy, David J. Jackowe, James L. Kochan, Bob McDonald, Eric Schnitzer, Robert A. Selig, Gregory Theberge, and Anthony Wayne Tommell, who, as always, were ready to help in every way.

Don Troiani
Southbury, Connecticut
February 2021

# FOREWORD

DON TROIANI'S PAINTINGS COLLECTED IN THIS BOOK AND THE ACCOMPANY-ing exhibit at the Museum of the American Revolution (October 2021– September 2022) provide one of the most reliable answers to a question that must intrigue anyone interested in the founding era of the United States: what did the American Revolutionary War actually look like? With photography still fifty years away from being invented, with painting in the early United States in its infancy, and with few professional artists trained in early America to witness and depict the battles and events, historians have had to assemble any visual impression of the period through bits and pieces of information, often layered and inevitably mixed with impressions of war from later periods or places where imagery was more prevalent.

For the importance of the American Revolutionary War—as a trial that shaped a new nation, engaged the lives of the diverse people of North America, Europe, and Africa, and established that a republic could beat the world's most powerful monarchy—the conflict has long been under-represented in art. Even artists of the classic era of illustration that came later in the late nineteenth century seem to have taken less interest in the American Revolution than in other modern conflicts, like the Amer-ican Civil War or the Napoleonic Wars, for example. There are dozens of images of Gettysburg or Waterloo for every one of Valley Forge. The images in this volume are the results of Don Troiani's unparalleled effort to correct that inattention with research-based depictions of the soldiers, sailors, other combatants, and civilians on all sides of the conflict.

Troiani's scrupulous research methods have included site visits, archi-val work, collecting original objects, and archaeology. The unique prob-lem of producing a piece of artwork pressed him to delve deeply into the study of the material culture of these preindustrial armies. His paintings have been some of the first secondary sources to publish new informa-tion about the material lives and physical experiences of combatants: the accurate shape of Continental Army cartridge boxes and canteens, the uniforms of some Loyalist forces, and the exact location and procedures by which the British Army laid down their arms at Yorktown, to name a few examples.

Avowedly not a partisan or fan of any particular group in the con-flict, Troiani shows an exceptional commitment to depicting not just the American side of the conflict, but also the British and German forces and their Native American allies. His works press us to question the accuracy of many familiar images of the American Revolution, like Paul Revere's engraving of the Boston Massacre or Howard Pyle's later depictions of British troops at Bunker Hill marching machinelike into certain disaster. Troiani's depictions of these same events suggest the role of politics and wishful thinking in the more familiar versions. Troiani describes his effort at an inclusive depiction of the American Revolution as patriotic. "I want to document the great scenes of American history," he says, "for the privilege of living here. It is something I can leave behind as a teaching tool."

Since its opening in 2017, the Museum of the American Revolution has been committed to a similar idea of patriotism and history. As the Museum's literature states, "a more diverse story is a more accurate story." The exhibition of Troiani's work at the Museum of the American Revolution grew from an idea to commission a painting that would capture some of the exceptional contributions to the American Revolutionary victory, and to the ongoing promise of the American Republic, of the men of African and Native American descent in the Rhode Island Regiment of the Continental Army. The scene is based on a memory of James Forten, a free Black man of Philadelphia, who saw the Rhode Island Regiment march down Chestnut Street, past the Pennsylvania State House (now called Independence Hall), and on to Virginia where it would fight at the Siege of Yorktown in 1781. In a letter Forten wrote to William Lloyd Garrison in 1831, he remembered that the vision of these "brave Men as ever fought" inspired him later to become an abolitionist. Commission of the painting was made possible thanks to generous support from the Washington-Rochambeau Revolutionary Route National Historic Trail of the National Park Service.

We soon realized that placing this painting in the context of Troiani's many other works on the Revolutionary War creates a whole greater than the sum of its parts. The populations at war were complex and dynamic, their motivations, tactics, and unit cultures various and diverse. We see the war in a new way. It takes on a vibrancy—red coats against blue sky and green forests—that might seem discordant with its grim realities. Its bloody severity includes combatants we might not expect, from Margaret Corbin at the guns of Fort Washington to Stockbridge Indian fighters in the grasses of what is now the Bronx. These surprises testify to the power of Troiani's art to confront the errors in our expectations and see the Revolutionary War with its far-reaching promise and bitter ironies.

Philip C. Mead
Chief Historian and Curator
Museum of the American Revolution

# 1

# LET IT BEGIN HERE

THE REVOLUTIONARY WAR BEGAN IN 1775 WITH A "SHOT HEARD ROUND THE WORLD."

Five years earlier, on March 5, 1770, the Boston Massacre had strained the already tense relationship between Americans and British troops stationed in the colonies. New England militiamen, over the next few years, stockpiled arms and ammunition and increased their training efforts. The courageous New Englanders proved professional and effective in battles at Lexington, Concord, and Bunker Hill, inflicting heavy casualties on the British Army and causing the British commanders to rethink their strategies.

The paintings in this chapter transport us to a chaotic night in Boston in 1770, a frosty April morning in Lexington, and a bright June afternoon on a hill overlooking Boston Harbor. They show the violent days that ignited the Revolutionary War.

# THE BOSTON MASSACRE, MARCH 5, 1770

THE BOSTON MASSACRE IS A DEFINING MOMENT for the years leading up to the American Revolution. Sparked by a barber's apprentice taunting a British officer over an unpaid bill, it flamed into battle as tensions escalated between the town's inhabitants and the soldiers of King George III's army who had arrived in Boston on October 1, 1768.

On March 5, 1770, Private Hugh White of the 29th Regiment of Foot stood guard before the Customs House in Boston. Having witnessed Edward Garrick verbally assault Captain-Lieutenant John Goldfinch, he reprimanded the youth with a strike to his head with his firelock. This ignited a fuse of retaliation. A "motley rabble of saucy boys, negroes and molattoes, Irish teagues and out landish jack tarrs" swarmed upon White with clubs and staves.[1] Overwhelmed, the sentry called out for relief.

As shown in this painting, the mob continued to grow and become more violent. Church bells began to ring. Corporal William Wemms managed to lead a guard of six grenadiers from the 29th Regiment to relieve the sentry. Unable to escape to the main guardhouse, they formed a semicircular line and leveled their bayonets at the breasts of their adversaries. Within moments, Captain Thomas Preston worked his way to take command.

Within the chaos, many individuals stood out. Henry Knox and Richard Palmes both approached Captain Preston and inquired if his men would fire upon the inhabitants. Benjamin Burdick, a Town House Watchman, struck a soldier's firelock with a Scottish broadsword.

As the crowd grew more and more agitated, a man in a dark, gold-trimmed suit walked behind the soldiers and encouraged them to fire. Without warning a shot rang out and more followed. Crispus Attucks, a sailor of African and Native American descent, fell to the ground.

After the smoke cleared that cold winter's evening, blood spattered the snow. Three men lay dead, a man and boy lay mortally wounded, six men were taken away to recover from their wounds, and a day of infamy was recorded in the annals of American history.

*Gregory Theberge*

### Artist Comment

The snow for this painting was posed after we had a storm here in Connecticut that produced the correct depth. Wearing a pair of replica eighteenth-century shoes, I tramped through the drifts and took photographs in the night. The greatest challenge was reconstructing the buildings in the background to their correct eighteenth-century appearance. I posed the models in the garage with artificial lighting *(above)* to replicate how the gun flashes would fall on the models.

**The Bloody Massacre**

*Courtesy of the Dietrich American Foundation*

Paul Revere's famous engraving of the Boston Massacre misrepresents the British soldiers as murderers who fired deliberately and in unison into a crowd of civilians. In reality, a swarm of Bostonians threw rocks and snowballs at the soldiers, who fired back in confusion and self-defense. Revere's engraving, distributed as stand-alone prints and on broadsides, inflamed Americans who demanded the removal of the British troops in Boston to protect the safety and liberty of the people.

# LEXINGTON COMMON, APRIL 19, 1775

AT ABOUT MIDNIGHT ON APRIL 19, 1775, Boston silversmith and alarm rider Paul Revere rode into the town of Lexington, Massachusetts, to alert Samuel Adams, John Hancock, and local minute man and militia companies along the way that British troops were on the march to Concord looking for cannon and other military supplies. Both Adams and Hancock had been at the Provincial Congress meetings in Concord that had recessed on April 15, a few days earlier, and were staying at the home of the Reverend Jonas Clarke in Lexington. Earlier in the evening, British scouts were seen riding through town on the way toward Concord to secure the way for the main body of troops. The men of Lexington knew something was going on prior to the alarm and had placed a guard around Reverend Clarke's house as a precaution in case the goal of the British troops was to capture the two provincial upstarts.

Soon after Revere's warning that the British troops were on the march, the bell in the town's belfry was rung to sound the alarm and scouts were sent toward Menotomy, just to the east of Lexington, to reconnoiter and report back. By two o'clock in the morning, forty-five-year-old Captain John Parker had formed his militia company on the common, approximately 130 men, and ordered them to load their muskets. After one scout had returned to town seeing no sign of the British troops, Captain Parker dismissed the militia to be recalled at the sound of sixteen-year-old William Diamond's drum. Some went home and others congregated at Buckman's Tavern, which was located just next to the common.

Unbeknown to Parker, there were actually some seven hundred elite British light infantry and grenadiers on the march to Concord, a route that would take them past the common in Lexington. They had placed six light infantry companies in the vanguard to take and hold the two main roads from the west into Concord. The six advance light companies were under the command of Major John Pitcairn of the marine detachment stationed in Boston.

As the front of the British column marched along the road through Menotomy and into Lexington, they began to see signs of militia movements. Alarm bells could be heard ringing, armed men moved about, and they began to wonder if the countryside had been alarmed. Soon they would capture the advance scouts that Captain Parker had sent to find the column as they moved into the outskirts of the town.

Finally, at about five o'clock in the morning, word did come back to Parker that the troops were close. He ordered the young William Diamond to beat his drum and assemble the militia. As shown in this painting, some seventy-seven men hastily formed on the common facing the road to Concord in two ranks. As the light infantry companies came onto the common at the double-quick march, Parker's militia company was still not yet completely formed. Things began to move at a faster pace, which would prove deadly to some of Parker's men.

Major Pitcairn rode onto the common calling on his troops not to fire, but to surround and disarm the assembled militia. A mounted British officer, probably Pitcairn, also ordered the rebels, as the British commanders referred to the American soldiers, to "Lay down your arms and disperse."[2] A shot rang out, possibly from one of Parker's men at a stone wall on the edge of the common; whether it was one of the militiamen, or the British light infantry, is lost to history. As the first shots were fired, the light infantry, with no orders to do such, "began a scattered fire," while Major Pitcairn and his other officers tried to regain control of the companies that had rushed forward firing and lunging at the militia with bayonets.[3]

According to Parker, seconds before the firing had begun, some of his men had started to disperse, and, as the firing began, "A number of our men were instantly killed and wounded."[4] The British officers re-formed their men, and as the smoke cleared, eight Lexington men were dead and another ten wounded. One of the men, Jonathan Harrington, had crawled back to the doorstep of his home just behind Parker's position on the common. For the British advance light infantry, one man had been wounded and Pitcairn's horse had also been hit.

The British then re-formed and marched off toward Concord. Parker's men removed their dead from the common, tended to their wounded, and prepared to exact retribution later in the day.

*Joel R. Bohy*

# The Royal Regiment of Artillery, 1775

Unlike British Army infantrymen, the four battalions of the Royal Artillery wore blue coats faced with red. Five companies of the 4th Battalion of Royal Artillery were stationed in Boston in 1775.

# 52ND REGIMENT OF FOOT, GRENADIER COMPANY, PRIVATE, 1775

THIS PRIVATE SOLDIER WEARS THE DISTINCTIVE bear-fur cap of the British grenadiers. The 52nd Regiment's grenadier company fought at the Battle of Lexington and Concord. They wore red coats faced with buff and trimmed with lace featuring a "red worm" and an orange stripe.

### British Grenadier Cap

*Troiani Collection*

The Latin motto "NEC ASPERA TERRENT" (not afraid of difficulties) decorates the front plate of this bear-fur British grenadier cap. These fur caps with metal plates replaced earlier wool cloth grenadier caps following the adoption of the Royal Clothing Warrant of 1768. Despite their appearance, these caps were quite light and collapsible for easy storage in a bag when not in use.

# MINUTE MAN, MASSACHUSETTS MILITIA, 1775

DRESSED IN A BROWN BROADCLOTH COAT, breeches, and waistcoat, this minute man clutches an old British musket with a wooden ramrod. Paid extra for their duty, the minute men of the Massachusetts militia trained to be ready at a moment's warning. The minute companies were well armed and equipped, every man with a musket and cartridge box or powder horn. Some companies were fully equipped with bayonets while others had swords or hatchets.

# Concord Bridge, the Nineteenth of April, 1775

Following an alarm that a column of British troops had marched out of Boston, by nine o'clock on the morning of April 19, 1775, some 450 men congregated on a rising pasture above the North Bridge leading out of Concord. Most of the men were from that town and the neighboring ones of Acton, Lincoln, and Bedford. At the same time, seven hundred British grenadiers and light infantrymen in Concord looked for military supplies and arms. The troops had already spilled the blood of Americans on nearby Lexington Green earlier that morning. Three British light companies from the 4th, 10th, and 43rd regiments assembled immediately below the gathering Massachusetts minute men and militia guarding the North Bridge and its approaches. As additional reinforcements arrived, Lieutenant Joseph Hosmer of Concord, acting as adjutant, began to organize the men. A meeting of officers was held to decide their next move. As companies formed into line, the men could not help wondering what might transpire. Would cooler heads prevail?

Colonel James Barrett rode along the line on horseback, cautioning the men not to discharge their arms, before joining the assembling officers. The men checked their muskets, wiping the locks of the guns to clear the moisture that rose on them from the early morning dew. As the officers debated their next move, smoke began to rise from the town center. The British troops had begun to burn what meager supplies they had found and the blaze had spread to the nearby town house and harness shop of Reuben Brown. Widow Martha Moulton, seventy-one years old, pleaded with British officers to send their men to help put out the fire. Reluctantly or not, the grenadiers splashed buckets of water on the burning buildings, adding to the smoke already billowing above the town.

The Acton Minute Company, commanded by Captain Isaac Davis, arrived on the field and took its position in the line with the other minute and militia companies. Davis, a gunsmith by trade, had ensured that most of the muskets and fowling pieces carried by his men were capable of mounting bayonets, and the majority of them also carried cartridge boxes. The flap of Private Thomas Thorp's box was decorated "on the outside by a piece of red cloth in the shape of a heart," presented to him earlier that morning by "Doctor Swift, as he saw I had none." Thorp noted that when he joined his company "some of them were putting powder (flour) on their hair" in keeping with a genteel, martial appearance.[5] The Acton company had been training in the art of war since November of the previous year, twice weekly, and the men seemed ready and eager to defend their homeland.

As the smoke rose above the town, it created a stir among the anxious men above the bridge and Lieutenant Hosmer impatiently barked, "Will you let them burn the town down?"[6] The men then had a grave decision to make: let the town burn, or march on the King's men and fight. Whether because of his bravery or because of his well-equipped and trained company, Captain Davis and his Acton men were placed in the front of the column. They marched in a column of two files during their descent toward the bridge, Lieutenant Colonel John Robinson of Westford, Major John Buttrick of Concord, and Captain Davis in the lead. The British light infantry holding the environs nearby retreated to their comrades stationed at the bridge.

Captain Walter Laurie of the 43rd Regiment's light infantry, in command of the ninety-six British soldiers—principally light infantry with a few volunteer officers tagging along—saw a "body of country people . . . on the heights . . . with shouldered arms to the number of about fifteen hundred—they halted for a considerable time looking at us, and then moved down upon me in a seeming regular manner." Facing overwhelming odds, Captain Laurie "determined to re-pass the bridge . . . retreating by division, to check their progress, which we accordingly did, lining the opposite side of the river with one company, to flank the other two in case of an attack."[7] As the minute men and militia companies got closer, the British troops began to pull some of the loose planks off the bridge to prevent a crossing. Major Buttrick called on them to stop, and the light infantry responded by firing a volley at the advancing Americans, most of the balls splashing in the river. A round from a second volley—better aimed—hit fifer Luther Blanchard. Buttrick yelled to his men, "Fire, fellow soldiers, for God's sake fire!"[8] The fire of the British troops had killed Captain Davis and Private Abner Hosmer and wounded a few others.

Drawn up in column in the roadway before the bridge, as shown in this painting, the few Americans that could aim without hitting their neighbors heeded Buttrick's command and returned fire. As the Americans deployed and more guns were brought to bear, the British light infantry withdrew in a panic toward the safety of a column of grenadiers that had marched out of town to reinforce them. As the redcoats evacuated Concord and its environs, they were followed and flanked by a swarm of angry, buzzing Americans from the nest they had disturbed. The British troops were stung badly on their retreat back into Boston, with some 73 officers and men killed, another 174 wounded, and some 26 missing or captured. April 19 began eight years of bloody conflict that resulted in the 1783 Treaty of Paris and the creation of a new nation, the United States of America.

*Joel R. Bohy and James L. Kochan*

***Artist Comment***
A visit to the actual site with Joel Bohy and Jim Hollister, Park Ranger at Minute Man National Historical Park, was a great experience for me. Reconstructing how the background appeared using period maps was almost as time consuming as painting the principal figures. Sometimes less significant parts of a painting that are taken for granted often garner the most attention.

# BATTLE OF BUNKER HILL

As men on Breed's Hill overlooking Boston watched on the afternoon of June 17, 1775, it appeared as if the entire might of the British Empire was about to be flung against their makeshift fort and outer works. The New Englanders had already endured the seemingly unendurable—since five o'clock in the morning the citizen soldiers withstood intermittent, massed cannonades from British Navy warships on the Charles River and the British batteries in Boston. British field artillery below the hilltop defenders also fired upon them. Miraculously, the 150 or so New England farmers, tradesmen, sailors, laborers, old men, and boys of European, African, and Native American ancestry suffered few casualties from the tremendous barrage. By three o'clock in the afternoon, the men thirsted for water. Some licked their cracked and dirt-ringed lips with dry, fur-like tongues while they handled their arms. The sound of drums and fifes reverberated in the air, as nearly two thousand British troops began their upward march against the armed colonists. The defenders only heard, at first, the red-coated soldiers advancing. The lower slope of the hill temporarily shielded the marching British troops. The spectacle of the armed array, combined with the conflagration

of Charlestown's burning buildings below, transformed the once-pastoral setting into a hellish scene worse than any described by fire-and-brimstone preachers. In the redoubt, Colonel William Prescott stood on the wall with his sword in hand, haranguing his men to hold their fire until the redcoats marched within killing range.

More than a thousand New England troops had been on this godforsaken hill since the previous night, working feverishly to fortify it before the light of dawn revealed their position to the British. The troops belonged to Colonel Prescott's, Colonel James Frye's, and Colonel Ebenezer Bridge's Massachusetts battalions and Captain Samuel Gridley's artillery company, supplemented by a party of two hundred men drawn from Brigadier General Israel Putnam's Connecticut regiment under Captain Thomas Knowlton. They had been paraded in their Cambridge camp for fatigue duty at six o'clock in the evening with arms, blankets, and a day's rations. By nine o'clock that night they began the march, accompanied by carts loaded with entrenching tools, to a destination known only to their senior officers. Colonel Prescott and Colonel Richard Gridley led the column. Both officers had seen prior military service—Gridley

**"Broad Arrow" Cannonball**
*Troiani Collection*
The "Broad Arrow" mark on this 12-pound iron cannonball signified it as property of the British Board of Ordnance. British guns on land and aboard ships in Boston Harbor "kept an incessant fire" of iron shot and shells on the New England troops at the Battle of Bunker Hill. British Major-General John Burgoyne, who witnessed the roar of the guns that day, described it as "one of the greatest scenes of war that can be conceived."[9]

**Connecticut Officer's Fowling Piece**
*Courtesy of Brian and Barbara Hendelson*
Captain Samuel McClellan of Connecticut, a French and Indian War veteran, probably carried this fowling piece when he fought at the Battle of Bunker Hill. Made by Massachusetts gunsmith Joel White in about 1775, the fowling piece was built to mount a bayonet. It features White's name on the lock plate and on the top of the barrel. Its serpent-shaped silver side plate bears McClellan's initials: "SMC."

had directed the successful siege operations against French-held Louisbourg thirty years earlier and now was the chief engineer of the "Grand Army" of the rebellious American colonies. Prescott had been an ensign during the French and Indian War and wore the old blue coat of the provincial regiment in which he had served. Under it, he wore a red waistcoat, homespun breeches, and blue stockings, with a sword slung high on his left side, carried in a waist belt slung over his right shoulder. As the sun rose in the sky, so did the heat, and the 6-foot-tall, bald-headed colonel shed his coat, as did others, donning a lightweight calico banyan or lounging robe in its stead.

Some of the older men had similar military experience, fighting years before on behalf of their king, rather than against his ministers as they did in 1775. Their weapons often had similar histories: "here an old soldier carried a heavy Queen's arm, with which he had done service at the Conquest of Canada twenty years previous, while by his side walked a stripling boy with a Spanish fusee not half its weight or calibre, which his grandfather may have taken at the Havana, while not a few had old French pieces, that dated back to the reduction of Louisburg."[10] Some old men sported long, full-skirted coats and waistcoats decades out of fashion, while here and there a fisherman or sailor

stood out in the short jacket, loose trousers, and round hat characteristic of a seafaring man. But by and large, most of the men were farmers and tradesman dressed in the plain, everyday work clothing worn in the field or shop.

At Charlestown Neck the column was met by Brigadier General Putnam and additional wagons with tools and materials. Charlestown was a triangular peninsula that was bounded by the Mystic River to the north and the Charles River to the south, on the opposite bank of which lay the north side of British-held Boston. The Neck was its lowest point, a narrow isthmus that often flooded at high tide, but most of the terrain was rolling and formed three distinct hills. The tallest of these hills was Bunker's Hill, which began at the Neck and reached 110 feet at rounded eminence. To counteract British plans to seize the heights that commanded Boston from the north side of the Charles River, it was decided that "Bunker's Hill, in Charlestown, be securely kept and defended."[11] This was the mission of Prescott's command. However, Breed's Hill, connected to the former by a narrow ridge, was closer to Boston, although only 75 feet high. An ad hoc council of war was convened on-site to debate the merits of erecting earthworks on the two positions and eventually, pressed by Gridley for a decision, Breed's Hill was selected—with the intention of erecting additional works on Bunker's Hill, time permitting.

As shown in this painting, Prescott and his officers urged the nervous men in the redoubt to hold their fire as the British advanced upon the Breed's Hill redoubt. When the order was given, a withering volley erupted from the earthen walls. The British received the "hottest fire they ever saw" and their line broke, only to be formed again for another attack.[12] Again their advance faltered against the unceasing,

and now unregulated, fire from the American position. Some of the British soldiers rushed into the ditch and flung themselves against the earthen embankment of the redoubt to escape slaughter, waiting for another British attack or a cessation of gunfire. Inside the redoubt, ammunition ran low. The British left wing, regiments now intermixed, reformed for a final charge that took them to the walls and over, receiving one final, but less lethal, fire from the defenders. The New Englanders pulled back to the north wall and attempted to flee the redoubt through its open back. The rearmost of the retreating Americans were put to the bayonet, and resistance collapsed along the entire hillside, since the redoubt fell. The assault was a victory for the British, but a Pyrrhic one. Hopes for a quick end to the "rebellion" were shattered by the determined American resistance and resultant heavy casualties among the British forces. Soon after, the battle on June 17, 1775, became mistakenly known on both sides of the Atlantic as "Bunker Hill."

*James L. Kochan*

### Artist Comment

My esteemed friend, the now deceased collector Richard Ulbrich, posed for this painting and brought some of his magnificent original New England flintlock fowling pieces, a few of which could have been used in the battle. My young nephew, Marc, is posed next to him.

# The Redoubt, Battle of Bunker Hill, June 17, 1775

With the break of dawn over Boston Harbor on June 17, 1775, the captain and crew of the HMS *Lively* discovered that the New England troops ringing Boston succeeded in throwing up an earthen redoubt and flanking breastwork on the heights of Charlestown peninsula during the night. As the King's ships and land batteries from Boston continued their bombardment of the freshly dug rebel works to their east, British commanders formulated plans to take the works erected on Breed's Hill by assault. By noon, approximately fifteen hundred British troops under the command of Major-General William Howe moved from Boston across the Charles River to Morton's Point at the confluence of the Charles River and the Mystic River, where they landed between one o'clock and two o'clock in the afternoon. Howe formed the troops in three successive lines on the rising ground, locally known as Moulton's Hill, east of the American defenses. The front line was composed of the army's elite flank troops: the light infantry and the grenadiers. Detachments from the 5th and 38th regiments formed behind them, while the third line was composed of troops drawn from the 43rd and 52nd regiments. The strongly manned rebel positions convinced Howe that he needed to apply for reinforcements. Howe and his men waited while a second embarkation took place, consisting of the companies of light infantry and grenadiers that had been left in Boston, along with the 1st Battalion of Marines and the 47th Regiment. These latter troops, under the command of Brigadier-General Robert Pigot, landed under enemy fire at the easternmost edge of Charlestown (a community contained to the south by the Charles River and to the north by Breed's Hill) and southeast of Howe's position. Fire from American sharpshooters on the edge of town impeded their progress forward, until Charlestown was set ablaze by fire from batteries in Boston.

It was not until nearly three o'clock that afternoon that Howe finalized the arrangement of his battle dispositions and began the attack on the Americans on Breed's Hill. The light infantry on the right of Howe's battle line advanced along the Mystic River beach to attempt to turn the left of the American line, while the grenadiers, supported by the four line battalions under Howe, attacked the center of the American line. Pigot's troops deployed as soon as they landed, in a flanking movement intended to force the American right and take the redoubt. The British lines advanced slowly,

**British Marine Belt Plate**

*Troiani Collection*

The enlisted men of the British Marines wore anchor-decorated brass plates, like this example, on the shoulder belts for their bayonets. Two battalions of the British Marines fought at the Battle of Bunker Hill. One officer described the battle as a "very fatal" action for the marines due to the heavy casualties they suffered.[13]

### Royal Welsh Fusiliers Hanger

*Museum of the American Revolution*

The brass hilt of this hanger is decorated with a crown over the three ostrich plumes of the Prince of Wales. Made for use by the 23rd Regiment of Foot, also known as the Royal Welsh Fusiliers, the hanger bears the German motto of the Prince of Wales: "ICH DIEN" (I serve). The 23rd Regiment's grenadier and light infantry companies fought at the Battle of Bunker Hill.

frequently halting as covering batteries of artillery fired. Howe soon encountered further difficulties in attempting to advance his line of battle, from "very high & strong fences of posts & railing . . . parallel to ye enemy's works [that] greatly impeded . . . passing them in a very hot fire."[14] Likewise, Pigot's left wing ran into similar problems, gaining "Ground on the Enemy but slowly, as the Rails Hedges & stone walls, broke [their formations] . . . and several Men were shot in the Act of climbing them."[15] Two assaults attempted by Howe's main line were thrown back under heavy enemy fire. The British forces attempted a final desperate assault. The 5th, 38th, and 52nd regiments in the center suffered heavy casualties from enemy fire, impeded and broken in their advance forward by swampy ground, brick kilns, and fields with fencing in front of the redoubt. Finally, they reached the relative shelter of the earthwork's ditch where "the enemy could not depress their arms sufficiently to do any execution to those

that were close under," but the men of the three regiments lost all order as they sought cover from the withering fire of the defenders.[16] To the right of them, some of the grenadiers succeeded in breaching the northern end of retrenchment at its curtain, contiguous to the northeast angle of the redoubt.

Meanwhile, the 1st Battalion of Marines and the 47th Regiment on the left nearly reached the southern wall of the redoubt, when they also received "a Check (tho' without retreating an Inch) from the very heavy and severe Fire from the Enemy in the Redoubt."[17] The beloved commander of the marines, Major John Pitcairn, lost his life at the head of his men in this attack, with a score of other officers and men killed or wounded. For a period of time, it seemed as if this combined, third assault had also failed. But the troops, enraged by the losses they suffered and "half mad with standing" exposed in the open like sitting ducks, were rallied by their officers. The

marines and the 47th Regiment "without firing a Shot" jumped into the ditch and scaled up and over the parapet of the redoubt.[18]

As shown in this painting, when the marines and 47th Regiment poured over the walls, the Americans—their ammunition now expended—attempted to retreat out of the rear of the redoubt. Many of the rearmost men, many with nothing left to defend themselves but clubbed muskets and fowling pieces, rocks, and bare hands, were cut off and killed. Among the slain was Doctor Joseph Warren, president of the Massachusetts Provincial Congress, who fought that day as a volunteer in the ranks armed with a fusil and sword, yet elegantly dressed in a light suit that included a fringed silk waistcoat. Marines and 47th Regiment soldiers, both clad in red uniforms with white facings, along with bearskin-capped grenadiers, sought to avenge lost comrades. "The Horror of the Scene within the Redoubt . . . streaming with Blood & strew'd with dead

& dying Men the Soldiers stabbing some and dashing out the Brains of others was a sight too dreadful" to behold, according to the adjutant of the marines.[19] In the course of the battle, 140 Americans were killed and another 301 wounded, 30 of whom the British took prisoner. The carnage of the battlefield revealed staggering losses on the part of the British: 226 killed and another 828 wounded, some of whom would later die. Major-General Howe regretfully admitted that "the success is too dearly bought" in this Pyrrhic victory.[20]

*James L. Kochan*

***Artist Comment***

The British models for this painting spent hours jumping down off a stone wall during the shoots. Their knees were quite sore afterward. As you can see from my palette *(above)*, I use a wide variety of colors and am a very sloppy worker.

# A Soldier of Lord Dunmore's Ethiopian Regiment, 1775

While the new Continental Army encircled British-held Boston, Virginia's Royal Governor Lord Dunmore worked to subvert rebels in the colony he governed. He offered freedom to enslaved men owned by rebels who were able and willing to bear arms and fight on behalf of the king. Dunmore formed many of these men into the Ethiopian Regiment. Some members, as shown here, wore coats of the British 14th Regiment of Foot, which was stationed at the time in Virginia.

# 2

# THE TIMES THAT TRY MEN'S SOULS

THE AMERICAN REVOLUTION NEARLY FAILED IN 1776.

In the months after the United States of America declared their independence from Great Britain, the British Army and British Navy nearly crushed the rebellion. The new Continental Army led by General George Washington lost control of New York City after a series of battles. The army dwindled in both size and spirit, and it appeared as if the Revolution had come to a quick end.

Three small battles in New Jersey at Trenton and Princeton, daring successes led by General Washington, helped the Revolution survive. As one Loyalist put it, the campaign made the American Revolutionaries "liberty mad again."[1]

These paintings of the battles of 1776 allow us to meet Margaret Corbin, Nathan Hale, George Washington, Alexander Hamilton, and the Hessians in the middle of the action.

# Nathan Hale, September 22, 1776

Eighty-two-year-old Continental Army veteran Asher Wright, even sixty years after last seeing Nathan Hale, accurately recalled the key flaws that yielded Hale's catastrophic foray into espionage in September 1776: "When he left us, he told me he had got to be absent a while, and wanted I should take care of his things. . . . He was too good-looking to go so. He could not deceive. Some scrubby fellows ought to have gone."[2] From appearance and character, the twenty-one-year-old schoolmaster was the diametrically wrong man for the job. The surviving written accounts of those who had known him portray a youth of flawless integrity, incapable of duplicity; he could not deceive.

Fate also played a role in Hale's destiny. Entering Yale at age fourteen, class of 1773, his closest classmate ties developed with fifteen-year-old Benjamin Tallmadge, who would, in 1775, be instrumental in Hale's entering the army and becoming two years thereafter General Washington's premier spymaster. After only two years of teaching, Hale was commissioned a lieutenant in Colonel Charles Webb's Connecticut Regiment, serving the rest of 1775 in the lines surrounding British-occupied Boston. By early 1776, now Captain Hale commanded a company of the 19th Continental Regiment.

Having seen no significant combat service by late summer, he chronically longed to make significant contributions to his country. From this desire for more action, Hale, shortly before September 1, transferred to the specialized unit known as Knowlton's Rangers.

After the late-August defeat on Long Island and mass evacuation to Manhattan, Washington's army was at great risk. British naval superiority was insurmountable, and a major attack to capture the city and defeat the Continentals was fully predictable. For Washington, the key questions were when and where that blow would fall; timely intelligence was essential. He turned to Colonel Thomas Knowlton, asking him to find a ranger-volunteer for a spy mission. Captain Nathan Hale was the single man to step forward.

Hale crossed the Long Island Sound from Norwalk, Connecticut—exchanging his uniform for a brown civilian suit—making landfall in the predawn hours of September 17. Unknown to him, the anticipated British attack had fallen upon Kip's Bay two days earlier, obviating the need for his hazardous mission! Hale's solo landing on Long Island was almost immediately reported by Loyalist agents to the infamous Major Robert Rogers, who, by the 19th, was personally observing Hale. On the 21st, Hale was arrested by Rogers and taken to British headquarters at the Beekman House, at today's First Avenue and Fifty-First Street in Manhattan.

The enormous evidence against Hale, including his full confession, made the outcome of whatever trial he received a fait accompli; he was an enemy officer-spy traveling in mufti, the universal penalty for which was ignominious death by hanging. Shortly after ten o'clock in the morning on Sunday, September 22, 1776, Hale was marched under guard the short distance south from the Beekman House to the British artillery park, opposite the Dove Tavern—at today's Forty-Fifth Street.

### Artist Comment

Although there are many stories about where Captain Hale was hanged, primary evidence makes it clear that the execution happened near where the United Nations is today, along First Avenue. Another legend about a young African American boy serving as the hangman is false as well.

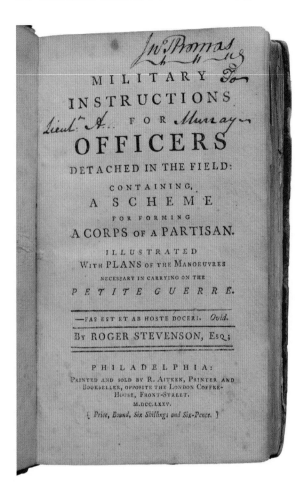

**Maryland Officer's Manual**

*Museum of the American Revolution*

Alexander Murray, a lieutenant in Smallwood's Battalion of Maryland troops, received this copy of *Military Instructions for Officers Detached in the Field* by Roger Stevenson as a gift in 1776. Printed in Philadelphia by Robert Aitken in 1775, it was the first book to be dedicated to General George Washington. Murray and many other American officers who served during the New York Campaign of 1776 carried copies of this manual in their knapsacks and chests. It served as a helpful reference, especially for officers with little or no prior military experience.

Hale's celebrated last words have long been grist for the debate mill. In reality, the purported "I only regret that I have but one life to lose for my country" can be reliably traced to no earlier than a 1799 history of New England influenced by William Hull, a close friend of Hale's from both Yale and the Continental Army.[3] Neither Hull nor any other friend of Hale—nor we—can know whether his last remarks included anything close to the famous lament. What is certain, though, is the eyewitness account of British Captain Frederick Mackenzie, whose diary entry for that fateful Sunday reports: "He behaved with great composure and resolution, saying he thought it the duty of every good Officer, to obey any orders given him by his Commander-in-Chief; and desired the Spectators to be at all times prepared to meet death in whatever shape it might appear."[4]

*Bob McDonald*

# Gentleman-Trooper, Hyde's Troop, Backus's Regiment of Connecticut Light Horse, 1776

In May 1776, Connecticut established five regiments of light horse as part of its militia forces. Major Ebenezer Backus led two of those regiments to reinforce the Continental Army in Westchester County, New York, in September and October 1776. General Washington dismissed them back to Connecticut on November 1 following their "faithful services" and lauded their "cheerfulness and alacrity they have shewn upon all occasions" as scouts for the army.[5]

**Rhode Island Officer's Sword**

*Courtesy of Brian and Barbara Hendelson*

The silver throat of this cuttoe's scabbard is engraved with its owner's name, J King, and that of its maker, goldsmith and jeweler John Gibbs of Providence, Rhode Island. Lieutenant James King carried this sword as a member of the 11th Continental Regiment in 1776, a unit of Rhode Islanders. While King struggled with sickness, his regiment fought in the battles around New York City, retreated across New Jersey, and served with distinction at the Second Battle of Trenton and the Battle of Princeton.

**New Jersey Soldier's Canteen**

*Troiani Collection*

Two iron hoops secure the staves of this wooden canteen. Made like a small barrel, the canteen bears the initials of its multiple owners and a paper label stating that it was carried during the Revolutionary War by a New Jersey soldier.

# A Grenadier of the 26th Continental Infantry, 1776

This Continental Army grenadier wears a wool cap decorated with a GW cipher, which stands for George Washington. The 26th Regiment served in New York in the fall of 1776. An original example of this regiment's grenadier cap survives in the collection of the Smithsonian's National Museum of American History.

# Mantz's Rifle Company of Frederick, Maryland, Flying Camp, 1776

In the summer of 1776, Captain Peter Mantz led riflemen north from Maryland to support the Continental Army in New York. They wore yellow hickory-dyed hunting shirts with green leggings and a bear-fur crest on their hats. Riflemen often dressed in linen hunting shirts of numerous colors ranging from white to purple or even black. According to General Washington, Mantz's men and other Marylanders "charged the Enemy with great Intrepidity" at the Battle of Harlem Heights on September 16.[6]

# HESSE-CASSEL GRENADIER OF THE 3RD GARDE REGIMENT, 1776

GRENADIERS OF THE 3RD GARDE REGIMENT served in the Hessian grenadier battalion led by Lieutenant Colonel Otto von Linsing. They fought at the Battle of Long Island on August 27, 1776, and later crossed the Hudson River into New Jersey following the capture of Fort Washington on November 16.

# MOUNTED TRUMPETER, BRITISH 17TH LIGHT DRAGOONS, 1776

WEARING A LACED WHITE COAT WITH RED FACings, the reversed colors of the British 17th Regiment of Light Dragoons, this trumpeter communicated orders to his fellow dragoons in battle. His cap is decorated with a skull over crossbones on its front plate.

# MARGARET CORBIN, FORT WASHINGTON

BY NOVEMBER 1776, THE LAST REVOLUTIONARY toehold on Manhattan was a rocky eminence that overlooked the Hudson or North River at the northern end of the island. Dubbed "Mount Washington" in honor of General George Washington, two regiments of Pennsylvania troops and militia from the Pennsylvania Flying Camp began construction of a fort (also bearing his name) and series of outworks upon it earlier that summer. Fort Washington was a pentagonal earthwork with a bastion in each corner. Built in conjunction with Fort Lee on the opposite (or New Jersey) bank of the Hudson, the two forts were strategically placed to impede Royal Navy efforts to ascend the river and to contain the British Army in the southern portion of Manhattan Island. In late October, additional reinforcements were detached to the fort, including the remnants of Colonel Hugh Stephenson's Maryland and Virginia Rifle Regiment. By November 14, it was clear that the British intended to attack the fort, and the garrison prepared for imminent battle. The riflemen were stationed on the northernmost end of the Mount Washington ridgeline, and two batteries were constructed at its apex, with supporting redans and firing lines scratched out of the rocky soil, all encircled

**Pennsylvania Officer's Epaulette**

*Troiani Collection*

This silver epaulette marked the rank of Henry Bicker Jr., who served as an ensign in the 3rd Pennsylvania Battalion in 1776. Bicker participated in the construction of Fort Washington on Manhattan Island, where he was captured along with his brother Walter during the battle there on November 16, 1776. Exchanged in 1778, Bicker returned to the Continental Army and served until the end of the war.

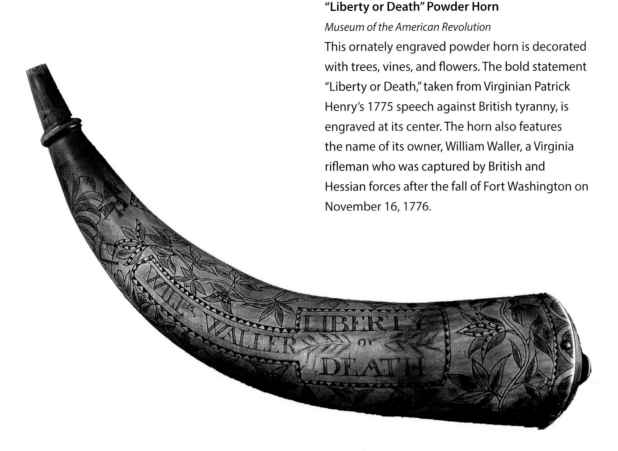

**"Liberty or Death" Powder Horn**

*Museum of the American Revolution*

This ornately engraved powder horn is decorated with trees, vines, and flowers. The bold statement "Liberty or Death," taken from Virginian Patrick Henry's 1775 speech against British tyranny, is engraved at its center. The horn also features the name of its owner, William Waller, a Virginia rifleman who was captured by British and Hessian forces after the fall of Fort Washington on November 16, 1776.

the illiterate young frontierswoman decided to follow her husband to war when he marched to New York as part of the Pennsylvania Flying Camp. Margaret likely served as a laundress to her husband's company, for which she probably was paid and drew half-rations in exchange for this labor. John Corbin was apparently one of a number of Pennsylvanians who arrived unarmed. It was decided that these troops were best utilized in the defense of the post by training them as matrosses to help work the many cannon placed in the fort and its outer batteries and redoubts. A Continental artilleryman supervised each gun crew.

Thus, on the morning of November 16, a young woman could be seen among the men in the northern redoubts, for Margaret refused to leave her husband's side even with a battle in the offing. The attack began at daybreak, when a huge cannonade commenced against the fort and its outworks from the numerous British batteries that surrounded the post. Tasked to take the northern strongpoint of redoubts was the Hessian corps under Lieutenant-General von Knyphausen, which formed up to attack in two columns under cover of a small woods. Both columns had to climb the steep slopes of the ridge while exposed to heavy rifle and cannon fire for nearly an hour, the left column especially suffering from the grapeshot fired by the cannon in the lower American battery. One Hessian soldier in the left column described the hellish experience as they "clambered up

by a wide abatis farther downslope. Manning the two fieldpieces of the main battery was a small detachment drawn from Captain William Pierce's company of Knox's Continental Regiment of Artillery, supplemented by men drawn from the Pennsylvania regiments and militia. Among the latter was John Corbin, who was accompanied by his wife of four years, Margaret Cochran Corbin.

Margaret Cochran was born on November 12, 1751, on a frontier farm near present-day Chambersburg, Pennsylvania. During an Indian raid in 1756, her father was killed and her mother taken captive, never to return home. She and her brother were adopted and raised by the uncle they had been staying with at the time of the raid. In 1772, Margaret married John Corbin and, apparently childless in 1776,

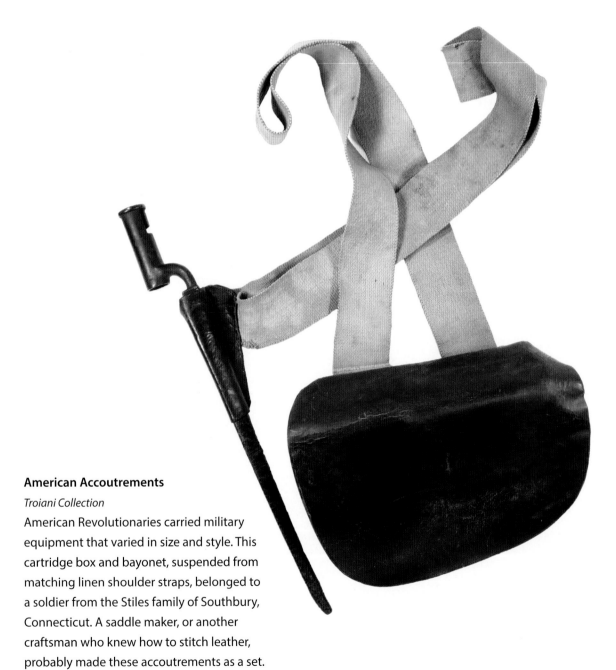

**American Accoutrements**

*Troiani Collection*

American Revolutionaries carried military equipment that varied in size and style. This cartridge box and bayonet, suspended from matching linen shoulder straps, belonged to a soldier from the Stiles family of Southbury, Connecticut. A saddle maker, or another craftsman who knew how to stitch leather, probably made these accoutrements as a set.

*Artist Comment*

The original site where this took place is near the Cloisters on Manhattan Island. The rocky slope (along the current West Side Highway) that the Hessians climbed up partly remains, as does their artillery position in Inwood Hill Park. The photograph *(right)* shows a Hessian grenadier model climbing the rocky slopes of "Manhattan" in my Connecticut backyard.

the hills and stone cliffs . . . one falling down alive, another being shot dead," as we "dragged ourselves upwards by grasping bushes up to the heights . . . we had a hard time of it." They finally reached the heights when "Colonel Rall commanded 'All who are my grenadiers, forward march!'"[7] As the Americans began a fighting withdrawal, Hessian Colonel Johann Rall and his hurrahing troops clambered into the American works and found, much to their amazement, the body of a woman among the fallen who had so valiantly defended that position.

As shown in this painting, Margaret Corbin, witnessing the death of her husband earlier in the action, took up his position at a cannon, fighting until she too was hit by three grapeshot fired from one of the enemy batteries. She suffered multiple wounds that mangled her left arm, jaw, and chest. As the Americans were pushed into the fort from the outer works, the position was no longer tenable. The garrison surrendered some hours later. Corbin was treated by surgeons and miraculously survived. Along with other wounded prisoners, she was later paroled and released.

Corbin was incapacitated by her wounds, no longer able to use her left arm. While she continued to draw military rations each day, she had no other means of support, and in 1779 Pennsylvania's government voted her thirty dollars to relieve her immediate needs. They then petitioned the Continental Congress to take her heroism and disabilities under consideration and provide additional succor. Congress responded by giving her an annual suit of soldier's clothing and later awarded her with a soldier's half-pay for life. Corbin, who lived until 1800, was the first woman pensioner of the United States. Revered as a war hero, she still proved more than a handful for the officers charged with her care and oversight, for she was infamous for her swearing, heavy drinking, and lack of hygiene—attributable both to her hard life, as well as the physical suffering that she endured for the remainder of her life. Corbin is buried on the grounds of the United States Military Academy at West Point, where a monument stands attesting to her valor and self-sacrifice.

*James L. Kochan*

# VICTORY OR DEATH, ADVANCE ON TRENTON

RECALLING THE DARK DAYS OF 1776, WHEN THE Continental Army retreated across New Jersey, a former army officer described the young Captain Alexander Hamilton's appearance: "I noticed a youth, a mere stripling, small, slender, almost delicate in frame, marching, with a cocked hat pulled down over his eyes, apparently lost in thought, with his hand resting on a cannon, and every now and then patting it, as if it were a favorite horse or a pet plaything."[8] Thomas Paine could not have chosen a more apt title than *The American Crisis* for his new pamphlet, for Washington's army was now rapidly approaching dissolution. After capturing Fort Washington and Fort Lee in mid-November, the combined British and German forces had driven the rebels westward across the entirety of New Jersey, from the Hudson River to the Delaware River. The army of the new United States seemed like a fleeing animal about to be bagged or slain. Captain Hamilton had a great deal about which to be lost in thought.

Most fortunately for the future of the United States, many among the Continental Army's top command had noticed Hamilton, the extraordinary West Indies–born youth during the prior year. Having become fully charged with revolutionary ardor, Hamilton dropped out of King's College—now Columbia University—to form a militia company in 1775. Offered staff positions by both Major General Nathanael Greene and Major General Lord Stirling, he deferred, seeking a combat command. In March 1776, he was commissioned to command the New York Provincial Company of Artillery. During the next nine months, his remarkable abilities were often observed by both General Washington and Continental Artillery commander Colonel Henry Knox.

But it was now December. The 3,500-man shadow of the Continental Army was in profound peril along the Delaware River's Pennsylvania shore, even its commander contemplating in private correspondence that "the game is pretty near up."[9] British commander Lieutenant-General William Howe, lacking the killer instinct, all but came to Washington's rescue by following the tradition at the time of suspending active campaigning in winter. Howe chose to pull his troops back into winter quarters and await a spring resumption of combat, leaving one brigade of German troops—the now intensely detested Hessians—to winter at Trenton, directly opposite the American rebels. With his innate aggressiveness and fully recognizing the depths of the crisis, Washington determined that the die must be cast. Trenton was his target.

From its initial planning, the attack on Trenton would rely heavily on the rapid deployment and firing of artillery. Washington designated Knox to design the order of march and the complex logistics to pull off the river crossing and nine-mile nighttime trudge under what would become a continual blizzard of snow, sleet, and intermittent heavy rain, all within continually howling nor'easter winds. Long after nightfall on Christmas Day, a total of eighteen guns, limbers, ammunition carts, and horse teams were wrested aboard repeated flatboat ferry crossings, surrounded by great masses of floe ice. Once on the New Jersey side, the artillery was strategically distributed among the infantry brigades in the line of march so to maximize the benefits of the Americans' lighter gun carriages and resultant swifter mobility in action.

Washington's goal was a December 26 first light attack on Trenton's garrison, but the operation was nearly four hours behind schedule as the mile-long column got underway in the worsening storm. The grueling efforts would yield an epic feat of determination. Most a hindrance to maintaining pace and schedule were the wheeled artillery pieces and their teams. Icy

roads made their journey even more difficult. Lacking mechanical brakes, great attention and straining sinew were required from the men on any substantive inclines or, more cruelly, declines along the way.

This painting captures the moment the Continental Army reached the Trenton outskirts. At far right, under their red banner, Virginia troops break into a run, closely followed by General Washington, his silver-hilted sword in hand. In the far-left foreground rides Captain Alexander Hamilton, directly following his New York artillery company, its two bronze 6-pound guns still tightly closed against the storm. Minutes later, under fire but atop high ground, Hamilton's guns blazed with solid shot and grapeshot down Trenton's King Street.

*Bob McDonald*

### Flag of the 8th Virginia Regiment

*Courtesy of Brian and Barbara Hendelson*

This silk flag formerly shimmered orange and gold in the sunlight when it was carried by the 8th Virginia Regiment during the middle years of the Revolutionary War. The remnants of the painted banner at the center of the flag include the regiment's number expressed as a Roman numeral: VIII. The 8th Virginia initially served in South Carolina in 1776 while other Virginia regiments campaigned with Washington's main army in New York, New Jersey, and Pennsylvania.

### Artist Comment

Although there are many versions of the crossing of the Delaware River, I thought it would be
interesting to show the final moments before
the assault on the town instead. A leaf blower
provided the wind effects during the many mod-
eling sessions. Each of the models who posed
for this painting was selected for his appearance and dressed and posed at the studio. The
in-progress photograph *(above)* shows *Victory or
Death, Advance on Trenton* with an overall gray
tone applied and the figures roughed in.

# Battle of Trenton, December 26, 1776

Diarist Corporal Philipp Steuernagel, 3rd Waldeck Regiment, reflected upon the extraordinary nature of the German force's arrival in America during the Revolutionary War:

"The Americans look us Germans over carefully, with distaste, because we have come to help steal their freedom. . . . The land, which so many poor and needy Europeans had made worthwhile, and . . . among those inhabitants love, truth, faith, and freedom of speech were to be found, were now, through war, to have their customs and well-being completely destroyed."[10]

In the first year following the Battle of Lexington and Concord, the contest between Britain and her colonies had remained a familial conflict. By those skirmishes' anniversary, however, it was clear that King George III would consider no reconciliation with his children-colonists short of their complete subjugation, for, by spring of 1776, he had contracted with six German principalities for an ultimate total of thirty thousand troops. So profoundly were Americans shocked by their father-monarch's unprecedented act that public opinion swung toward the previously unlikely aim of national independence. By the first week of July, their declaration to the world's nations justifying that great stride included in its bill of royal indictments that: "He is at this time transporting large Armies of foreign Mercenaries to compleat the works of death, desolation and tyranny . . ."

The German troops became central to the 1776 campaign aimed at destroying Washington's army. At Long Island, Kip's Bay, Harlem Heights, White Plains, and the capture of Fort Washington, Continental Army and militia troops were humiliatingly bested by European professionals. From this combat superiority, atop an innate animus toward upstart rebels, the redcoats and their Hessian allies developed a denigrating contempt for such "country clowns." Concurrently, American military and supporting civilian morale plummeted. During late November, with enemies in close pursuit, Washington led a dwindling remnant of his army across New Jersey and toward sanctuary behind the Delaware River; his less optimistic moments indeed led him to write: "I think the game is pretty near up."[11]

The British command opted for winter quarters, leaving the rebel army's destruction to await a spring campaign. A string of outposts in New Jersey served to remind Washington of the British presence. The British assigned three Hessian regiments, the Rall Grenadier Regiment, the Knyphausen Fusilier Regiment, and the Lossberg Fusilier Regiment, to garrison the town of Trenton. The garrison brigade was

**Hessian Hanger**

*Troiani Collection*

A FL cipher decorates the blade of this Hessian hanger, or short sword. FL stands for Friedrich II, Landgrave of Hesse-Cassel. Infantrymen in the Hessian Knyphausen, Rall, and Lossberg regiments carried hangers like this one at the Battle of Trenton.

### Hessian Cap Plates

*Colonel J. Craig Nannos Collection*

The United States Army Corps of Engineers found these brass Hessian cap plates in the mud of the Delaware River in the early 1900s. Hessian fusiliers, including those of the Knyphausen and Lossberg regiments who fought at Trenton, wore caps decorated with plates like these. Massachusetts fifer John Greenwood remembered seeing fellow Continental soldiers take brass caps from the dead and captured Hessians after the Battle of Trenton: "With these brass caps on it was laughable to see how our soldiers would strut—fellows with their elbows out and some without a collar to their half-a-shirt, no shoes, etc."[12]

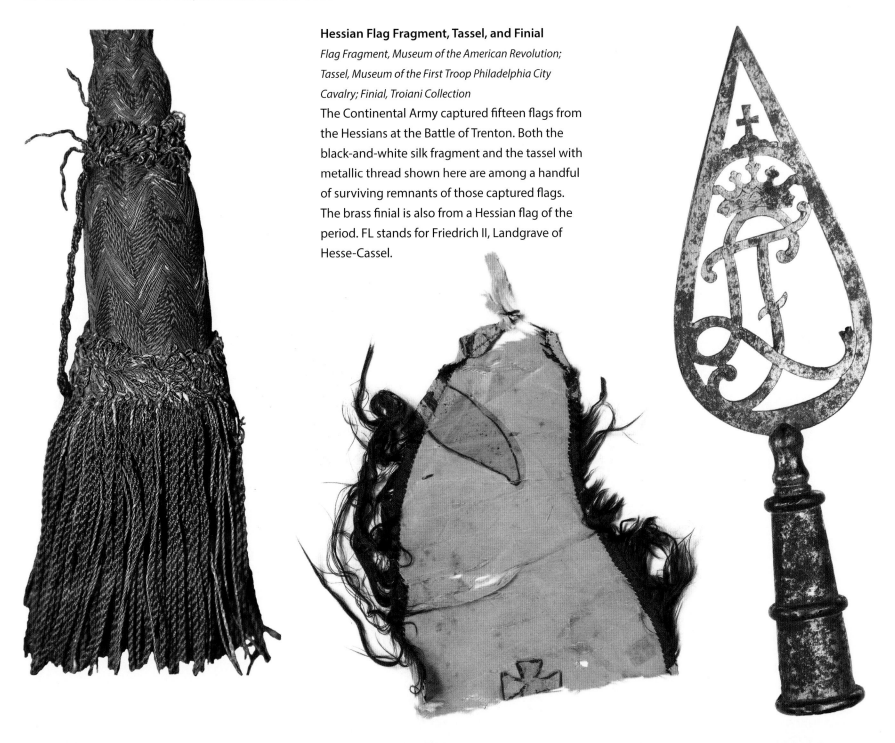

**Hessian Flag Fragment, Tassel, and Finial**

*Flag Fragment, Museum of the American Revolution;*
*Tassel, Museum of the First Troop Philadelphia City*
*Cavalry; Finial, Troiani Collection*

The Continental Army captured fifteen flags from the Hessians at the Battle of Trenton. Both the black-and-white silk fragment and the tassel with metallic thread shown here are among a handful of surviving remnants of those captured flags. The brass finial is also from a Hessian flag of the period. FL stands for Friedrich II, Landgrave of Hesse-Cassel.

**German Musket**

*Troiani Collection*

The Continental Army captured about a thousand muskets from the three Hessian regiments that surrendered following the Battle of Trenton. This German-made musket from the period, with its 41-inch-long, .72 caliber barrel, is comparable in size to the British Pattern 1769 Short Land musket.

commanded by fifty-year-old Colonel Johann Rall, a rough-hewn but successful combat officer with a remarkable thirty-six years of army experience. During their brief to-date service in America, these regiments had come to fully exemplify "Hessians," with savage battle performances and a growing reputation for plundering and abusing civilians. Placed at the northern-most position along the Delaware, Rall's Brigade was to manage a key hot zone amid the long line of occupation. Since arriving one week before Christmas, their position had been probed, harassed, and disrupted by near-daily forays of local militia and patrols of Continentals from their camp across the river.

Diarist Private Johannes Reuber of the Rall Grenadier Regiment recorded a small attack by the Americans on December 22: "A detachment at the Delaware was attacked by Americans who crossed . . ., set some houses on fire, and then retreated back across . . ."[13] A few days later, on Christmas night, Washington sprung his masterstroke. Following an arduous night-time crossing of the Delaware on December 25, the Continental Army marched to attack Trenton early in the morning on the 26th.

As shown in this painting, the Hessians quickly became overwhelmed at the Battle of Trenton because they were both outnumbered and outgunned. The battle left Colonel Rall (on horseback at center) with a mortal wound. Private Reuber described the attack:

"At daybreak, the Americans . . . fired on our outposts. At the first salvo, we turned out . . . to form and prepare our battle formations. Now the rebels pressed in on us. . . . the Americans charged Colonel Rall's quarters, overran it, and took the cannons from the regiment. Then Colonel Rall charged with his grenadiers. . . . we took our cannons and retired into the fields. Now Colonel Rall commanded, 'All

those who are my grenadiers, charge!' and they stormed against the city as the Americans retreated before us. However, after we had entered the city, the rebels, in three lines, marched around us and as we again tried to retreat, they again brought seven cannons into the main street. . . . If the colonel had not been so seriously wounded, they would not have taken us alive. . . . in the end, all was lost."[14]

As one among about nine hundred prisoners, Private Reuber was quickly marched to and across the Delaware River, and then on to a prison on the outskirts of Philadelphia. Colonel Rall died of his wounds that evening. American Revolutionaries, nearly all astonished by the victory, rejoiced.

*Bob McDonald*

**Artist Comment**

I must admit that I cannot resist the opportunity to paint Hessian uniforms, which are among my favorites. To prepare for this painting, I did a huge amount of research to make sure the material culture details were as accurate as possible, particularly with the drummer.

# 2ND BATTALION PHILADELPHIA ASSOCIATORS, 1776

WITH A BUCK TAIL IN HIS HAT, THIS PHILADELphia Associator wears the brown and red coat of the city's 2nd Battalion. The Philadelphia Associators painted their battalion number in Roman numerals on the flaps of their cartridge boxes. Painter Charles Willson Peale served as a lieutenant in this voluntary militia battalion, which fought at the Battle of Princeton.

# WASHINGTON AT THE BATTLE OF PRINCETON, 1777

LEARNING THAT GENERAL GEORGE WASHINGTON and his tattered army once again occupied Trenton, New Jersey, British Major-General Charles Cornwallis set out for that town with 5,500 picked troops on January 2, 1777, leaving behind the 4th Brigade as a rear guard at Princeton. Cornwallis was determined to capture the Continental Army that had eluded him far too many times in the past. Washington's army had most recently escaped by crossing the Delaware River back into Pennsylvania following their successful attack on the Hessian garrison at Trenton. On the morning of January 2, Washington, informed that Cornwallis was only eight miles distant, sent forward some of his best troops to delay the British advance column. Those troops held the British at bay for nearly three hours before being pushed back to the northern edge of Trenton, where another holding action was fought. Meanwhile, Washington's main body took up a strong defensive position on a ridge overlooking Assunpink Creek south of the town.

That evening, as the two armies opposed each other, Washington faced perhaps his greatest dilemma—to stay and fight the next day or to attempt another crossing of the Delaware River with an enemy in close pursuit.

Both options appeared very likely to result in the annihilation of his army, and with it, the prospects of survival for the fledgling United States of America. However, a third option was proposed and accepted during a war council: a withdrawal under cover of darkness and a forced march around the British left flank to strike at the British rear in Princeton. After leaving a rear guard to tend blazing fires and dig entrenchments to deceive the eyes and ears of the British outposts at Trenton, the army reached Stony Brook on the outskirts of Princeton at daybreak on the 3rd. Still undetected, Washington divided his force; the main column wheeled to the right and moved up a little-known route toward the town, while the left-hand or flanking column marched along the creek bank. Its mission: to secure the bridge on the main Princeton-Trenton road, thereby blocking retreat to, or reinforcement from, that quarter.

Meanwhile, Lieutenant Colonel Charles Mawhood of the 17th Regiment of Foot, the British commander at Princeton, had already marched out of Princeton before daybreak with most of his troops, under orders to join Cornwallis at Trenton. Leaving behind the 40th Regiment with some light dragoons for the town's defense, Mawhood marched southward along the Princeton-Trenton road with his own regiment, the 55th Regiment, two troops of light dragoons (one dismounted), and his field artillery, along with small detachments of grenadiers and Highlanders. The head of his column had already passed over Stony Brook when the opposing forces discovered each other.

Brigadier General Hugh Mercer, with approximately 350 picked men at the head of the left-hand American column, mostly Pennsylvania, Maryland, and Virginia riflemen supported by musket-armed infantry, pushed for the high ground to the north. The move gave them an ideal strongpoint from which to enfilade the British troops still strung out along the road. As they moved up the eastern slope, they passed the farmhouse and barns of William Clarke and marched into his orchard, forming a line of battle. In the meantime, Mawhood pushed his own men up the opposite slope, racing for the same high ground. He placed two fieldpieces supported by the grenadiers on his right flank, with the 17th Regiment composing his center and the dismounted dragoons on his left, dispatching most of the 55th Regiment back to reinforce the threatened town. The

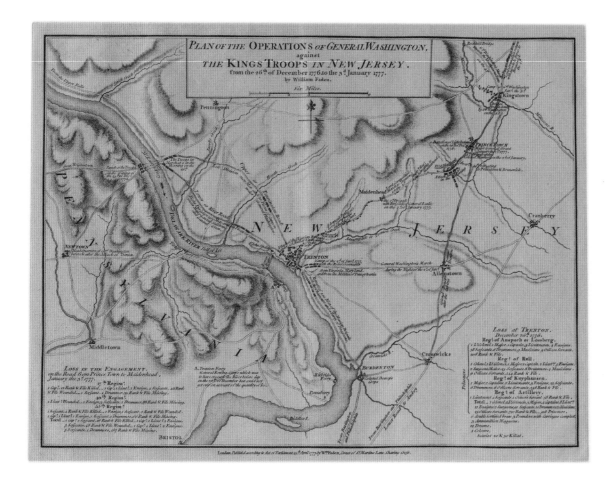

**Trenton-Princeton Campaign Map**

*Museum of the American Revolution,*

*Gift of Richard H. Brown*

Called the "10 Crucial Days" by historians, the period between December 25, 1776, and January 3, 1777, helped to save the American Revolution from a quick defeat. This British map documents the three battles, two at Trenton and one at Princeton, that took place in those ten days. General Washington's army crossed the Delaware River three times and marched well over thirty-five miles in that period to emerge victorious from the campaign.

Americans held their fire until the British stood within forty yards, even though some of the British troops had already fired (but with little effect, their shots largely high or wild). Mercer's troops let loose a withering discharge of rifle, musket, and cannon fire, which wreaked devastation upon the British right. A second American volley caused further destruction, leaving more than half of the roughly thirty grenadiers and many of the British officers now killed or wounded. Mawhood pushed the 17th Regiment onward in a bayonet charge. The sight of cold steel was too much for most of the Americans—few being armed with bayonets— and they broke and ran. Mercer himself fell as a round of grapeshot took off the foreleg of his horse and wounded him in the groin. He was then overtaken at the fence line by enraged British troops who stabbed him repeatedly with their bayonets when he refused to beg for quarter.

Colonel John Cadwalader's brigade of brown-clad Philadelphia Associators arrived on the scene and marched up to Clarke's farm, firing by platoons as they advanced. Mawhood's men turned a captured cannon on them and the grapeshot plowed into one of the foremost platoons of the 1st Battalion of Philadelphia Associators, killing Lieutenant Anthony Morris and some of his men. The sight of Mercer's retreating regulars and the blood of comrades proved too much for the volunteer militia, parade-ground trained, but devoid of combat experience. Some platoons broke and ran, while others withdrew in more or less orderly fashion to the safety of a woods in their rear.

As shown in this painting, Washington, accompanied by part of his staff, rushed from the main American column toward the sound of the guns to their left. Assisted by Colonel Cadwalader and other officers, he rallied the Associators and many of Mercer's troops, calling on them to advance toward their opponents. Washington led them in a charge against the right of Mawhood's line, with his men firing by platoons. At the same time, Colonel Daniel Hitchcock deployed his New England troops—rushed over from the main column—against the British left. The Yankee troops, admitted one Associator officer, "were the first who regularly formed" and withstood the fire from the British troops, as musket balls "whistled their thousand different notes around our heads."[15] Threatened with encirclement and having suffered more than a hundred casualties, Mawhood and his remaining 240 men resolved to retreat to the west, covering a wide arc of twenty miles until reaching Cornwallis.

Washington pushed his men up the main road to Princeton against the British force still in town. After a brief resistance, the British abandoned the town and retreated in broken order. The Continental Army's commander in chief, at the head of the 1st Troop of Philadelphia Cavalry and some rifle troops, stayed close on their heels in pursuit. Washington, according to one eyewitness, called out that "It is a fine fox chase, my boys!" as they rounded up some fifty British stragglers, in addition to the two hundred who surrendered in town.[16]

*James L. Kochan*

## Artist Comment

The American Revolution could have easily ended at Princeton had General Washington been killed leading his men. While most paintings of him are fairly static, showing Washington thinking or praying, I wanted to depict him in motion as the vibrant leader he was.

# Ferguson's Corps of British Riflemen, 1777

Wearing green coats and carrying their newly designed breechloading rifles with 25-inch-long bayonets, a group of Captain Patrick Ferguson's riflemen helped to lead the attack at the Battle of Paoli on September 20–21, 1777. Compared to muskets, which could be fired four times per minute, Ferguson rifles could be fired up to six times per minute with better accuracy.

# BRITISH 17TH LIGHT DRAGOON PRIVATE, PHILADELPHIA CAMPAIGN, 1777–1778

THE 17TH REGIMENT OF LIGHT DRAGOONS WAS one of two regiments of British light dragoons that served in America during the Revolutionary War. This dragoon wields his saber, but he is also armed with pistols and a carbine, the latter of which could be used when fighting dismounted. He wears a green jacket instead of his red regimental coat, a detail based on a 1782 painting of the Battle of Germantown that shows a member of the 17th Light Dragoons.

# 3

# VICTORY IN THE NORTH

IN MID-JUNE 1777, THE BRITISH LAUNCHED A PLAN TO BRING THEIR CANada Army into the war's American theater by reclaiming northern New York forts and capturing the City of Albany. In October 1777, the plan met its ultimate defeat at Saratoga.

The Saratoga Campaign engulfed the waterways and wilderness of New York and western Vermont. Fighting ranged from Lake Champlain to the Mohawk River Valley to the Hudson Highlands. The main British invasion force, about eight thousand British, German, Native American, Canadian, and Loyalist troops and camp followers led by Lieutenant-General John Burgoyne, left Montreal and set its sights on reaching Albany. They never made it. On October 17, Burgoyne's army surrendered to the Northern Army, a department of the Continental Army, under the command of Major General Horatio Gates. A rejoicing Massachusetts officer, Colonel Jeduthan Baldwin, wrote about the triumph: "A more compleat victory you could not wish for."[1]

The victory at Saratoga sent reverberations across America and across the Atlantic. France, emboldened by the news, formalized its military alliance with the United States. The Continental Congress commissioned a gold medal to celebrate the victorious Major General Gates. A member of the British Parliament regretted the defeat: "it is a disgrace which this nation never can recover."[2]

The paintings in this chapter show the drama of some of the key battles of the Saratoga Campaign. One shows Oneida Indians battling fellow Iroquois in the woods at Oriskany. Another captures the colorful uniforms of the Brunswick dragoons, part of Burgoyne's army, at Bennington. A third painting portrays the famed riflemen of the Continental Army who battled at Freeman's Farm and Bemus Heights. Together, these images help us grasp the momentous campaign on a more personal level.

# The Oneida at the Battle of Oriskany, August 6, 1777

The ambush was perfectly placed: four miles from Fort Schuyler, the dirt road through the mature forest snaked down to a ravine (over which a log-bed causeway had been laid in the past to make it passable by wagons during wet weather), before rising again and then coming to yet another ravine. Between the two ravines, the road was closely hemmed in by standing hemlock and other trees—broken at one point by a large deadfall created by an earlier tornado. On the heights above the second ravine, the light infantry company of the King's Royal Regiment of New York was placed to block the advance guard of the coming Revolutionary militia. Supporting the green-coated Loyalists was a small detachment of Hesse-Hanau Jäger, also dressed in green. On the high ground commanding one side of the road between the two ravines, it is said that their Native American allies (composed of warriors from the Seneca Nation and Cayuga Nation, plus Canada and Lake Indians and some Loyalist rangers) had carefully concealed themselves in anticipation of the pending assault on the main body of the rebel column of Americans. Closing the trap in the rear would be Mohawk Nation war captain Joseph Brant and his warriors. Now it was just a matter of quietly and patiently waiting for their prey during the rising heat and humidity of this August morning.

The approximately eight hundred men of the Tryon County Militia as well as the Oneida Nation warriors said to number sixty were strung out in a column extending for approximately one mile. That day the Oneidas were under the command of war captains Thawengarakwen (Honyery Doxtater) and Henry Cornelius Haunnagwasuke. The group was hampered by the narrow track and a slow-moving baggage train of ox-drawn wagons and carts near its rear. The militia had set out from their rendezvous at Fort Dayton two days earlier to relieve the beleaguered garrison of Continental regulars at Fort Stanwix (which had been recently renamed Fort Schuyler) before it was fully encircled. This strategic post was the gateway to the Mohawk River Valley and if it fell to the invading force of British and Loyalist troops and their Native American allies, the entire valley would be at their mercy. The previous night, the militia had encamped outside the Oneida town of Oriska, where they first learned that the fort was now besieged. Setting out early in the morning, they were only four miles from their ultimate goal and it was not quite ten o'clock in the morning. However, rather than utilizing the superior woods-skills of their Oneida allies on the flanks and in advance, most of the Oneida warriors marched in a body behind the lead regiment of militia.

Suddenly, before the supply train had fully crossed the first ravine, a shot rang out from near the center. The trap had been sprung, but too soon—either the premature discharge of an inexperienced young ambusher's gun or perhaps a discovery-warning shot fired by an alert flanker. In a matter of seconds, the scattered barks of squirrels were replaced with that of hundreds of muskets, fowling pieces, and rifles. Clouds of acrid, black-powder smoke enveloped the forest understory. Brigadier General Nicholas Herkimer, the fifty-year-old militia commander, was near the head of the column when a ball went through his horse and exited, shattering his leg and wedging it beneath the collapsed and dying horse. Dragged free and carried back to a safer position, he continued to direct his men as the battle soon developed into close hand-to-hand combat. After the initial shock wore off, the militia fought back valiantly, later taking advantage of the tree cover in the same fashion as their enemy had earlier, often fighting in teams of two—one firing while the other reloaded. Resolute Oneida warriors

such as Blatcop moved quickly into the woods, the best defense being offensive hit-and-run tactics. In the ensuing struggle, he broke the arm of one attacker with his tomahawk before dispatching him with a mortal blow; other Oneidas were not as fortunate, and the blood of those killed commingled on the ground with that spilled by their allies and enemies alike. The powerful Thawengarakwen fought valiantly, according to one account, killing at least nine warriors before taking a ball in his wrist. As portrayed in this painting, he fought on at close quarters, wielding a tomahawk while his wife Tyonajanegen (Two Kettles Together), who had accompanied him with the column, reloaded his fusil for him.

The fighting continued obstinately on both sides and with the opening surprise advantage squandered, the tide began to shift as the Revolutionaries tightened their defense cordon and fought back with effect. To counter this, the King's Royal Regiment of New York and the Jägera mounted a valiant, but ultimately futile, bayonet charge against the militia, suffering numerous casualties. Unobserved during the heat of battle, the sky darkened and a torrential downpour of rain was unleashed, providing nearly an hour's respite from the fierce fighting. Once the storm had passed, the conflict was renewed—first, a major onslaught against the American positions, which soon boiled down into a series of small, bloody localized skirmishes. With both sides having suffered heavy casualties, ammunition began to run low and exhaustion set in. Finally, as if almost by mutual consent, the daylong battle ended with the attackers withdrawing to their camps. Both sides claimed victory, but in reality, the Battle of Oriskany was largely a stalemate. While the ambush successfully prevented the relief of the besieged Fort Schuyler, the events of the day ultimately contributed to the abandonment of the siege by Lieutenant Colonel Barry St. Leger's army and its subsequent retreat from the Mohawk River Valley. For the Haudenosaunee (Iroquois Confederacy), sides had been taken and blood spilled. The Oneidas stood firm with the American Revolutionaries, but at great cost as they battled fellow nations of the Haudenosaunee.

*James L. Kochan*

### Artist Comment

Forest battles are tricky to paint due to the difficulty of trying to create a center of interest that is not obscured by smoke. Woodlands of that time were made up of large primary growth trees with a heavy canopy and little underbrush. Only filters of light could poke through. I try to place these filters of light where they will highlight centers of interest. I live in an area with heavy dark old forests and I just painted the trees larger than they are today.

# Hesse-Hanau Jäger, 1776–1777

A ninety-man company of Hesse-Hanau Jäger served in Lieutenant Colonel Barry St. Leger's diversionary force that invaded the Mohawk River Valley. They fought at the Battle of Oriskany. On campaign, one Jäger officer described that the company's worn-out coats "faded to brown with not a shade of green noticeable."[3]

# Brunswick Broadswords, The Brunswick Dragoons at the Battle of Bennington

Hessians. The word is synonymous with the tens of thousands of German soldiers hired by Britain during the American Revolutionary War. Because the British Army was made up of volunteers, and because too few Britons and Irishmen were willing to join, the British ministry sought assistance from states within the German Empire. The heads of six states ultimately agreed to lease their soldiers to fight in America, the first being Carl I of Herzogtum Braunschweig und Lüneburg (the Duchy of Brunswick and Lunenburg). The 4,300 troops borrowed from Brunswick by Britain and sent to Canada in 1776 were Brunswickers, not Hessians, a minor regional distinction that most Americans did not care to make.

One of few German cavalry corps deployed to North America during the war was Brunswick's Dragoon Regiment Prinz Ludwig. Named after Duke Carl I's younger brother, the regiment numbered about 330 officers and soldiers divided into four squadrons commanded in the field by Lieutenant Colonel Friedrich Baum. The British-Brunswick treaty stipulated that this light cavalry regiment would be deployed to America without horses and employed as infantry. Once landed in Canada in June 1776, the dragoons were placed on garrison duty and intensely drilled, so much so that the German commanding general, Friedrich Riedesel, lauded Baum's training regimen and his dragoons' prowess.

The dragoons retained a strange mix of cavalry and light infantry trappings. The soldiers continued to wear their enlarged cavalry hats and coats decorated with white shoulder aiguillettes that advertised their elite status. Most striking were the large cavalry broadswords carried by all officers and other ranks. Conversely, the soldiers' firearms were light, small-caliber carbines retrofitted to mount socket bayonets, a necessary infantry armament. Commensurate with their lightweight small arms were the diminutive buff leather cartridge boxes, each of which carried a paltry ten rounds of ammunition. Well trained and disciplined, the regiment was suited for skirmishing but not for sustained combat.

The Dragoon Regiment Prinz Ludwig formed part of the army commanded by Lieutenant-General John Burgoyne during the Saratoga Campaign of 1777 and was charged with guarding headquarters. In August, Burgoyne selected Baum for a special assignment—he would march most of his dragoons and other combatants, nearly seven hundred in all, southeast to Bennington, Vermont. There, he

### Brunswick Dragoon Officer's Broadsword
*Troiani Collection*

Officers of the Dragoon Regiment Prinz Ludwig from Brunswick carried long broadswords at the Battle of Bennington. The Dragoon Regiment Prinz Ludwig served as infantrymen in America, but they still carried arms and equipment appropriate for fighting on horseback. This sword's gilt-brass hilt features interlocking Cs, which stand for Carl I, Duke of Brunswick. Some of the Brunswick dragoon broadswords captured at Bennington were reissued to the Continental Army's 2nd Regiment of Light Dragoons.

would capture the Continental stores located in the town and proceed to Albany, New York, where Burgoyne would meet him in two weeks. Baum set off and arrived at Walloomsac, New York, located only miles from Bennington, on August 14, but Brigadier General John Stark's New England militia and rangers stood in his way. Baum requested reinforcements and dug in, deploying his dragoons on top of an enormous, steep hill and at a bridgehead located near its base. Two days later, Stark attacked.

It did not take long for the New Englanders to overwhelm Baum's positions and rout the defenders. In this painting, Baum's panic-stricken, mustachioed dragoons and musketeers from the Brunswick Infantry Regiment Specht tumble down the steep, towering hill in the face of Stark's onslaught, while a wounded drummer beats to rally as many of the fleeing soldiers as possible. With their scanty ammunition expended and the militia coming on fast, Baum, with drawn broadsword, orders his dragoons to sling their guns, draw their blades, and charge at the enemy. Together, they surged forth across the open fields before them, chased by Stark's militia toward the nearby Walloomsac River. It was not long before Baum fell, mortally wounded. The survivors surrendered. A last-minute arrival of reinforcements sent by Burgoyne to bolster Baum retreated after a sharp firefight.

So ended one of the most decisive battles of the entire war. In the end, Burgoyne's gamble cost him over 900 officers and soldiers, 670 of whom were in American captivity. The Dragoon Regiment Prinz Ludwig was obliterated, having lost about 30 killed and 195 captured of the 230 present. Burgoyne was forced to halt his mid-August advance upon Albany as he now had to wait upon his lengthy supply train, a process that stymied his army for a full month. This delay alone was the single most important contributing factor in bringing about the final, decisive showdown of the campaign—the Battles of Saratoga.

*Eric Schnitzer*

### Artist Comment

Owning two original Brunswick dragoon swords, I felt compelled to use them in a painting. The cartridge box in this painting was reproduced from the sole surviving original, as was the sword belt, which was captured at Bennington. Although it is costly to have these objects reproduced for a single painting, they contribute realistic detail that working from my imagination doesn't provide. My nephew Kian *(above)* posed for one of the Brunswick dragoons. It was a long, hot day, as you can see! I also had a coat with all the leather accoutrements *(left)* made for the dragoon drummer.

# FREEMAN'S FARM

THE BRITISH ARMY WAS A FIGHTING FORCE serving both the Kingdoms of Great Britain and Ireland. Irish regiments of the British Army were those in the service of the Irish kingdom, most of which were garrisoned on the Emerald Isle. One such regiment that served in America during the Revolutionary War, the 62nd Regiment of Foot, is shown here on September 19, 1777, at the Battle of Freeman's Farm.

Commanded in the field by a Scotsman, Lieutenant-Colonel John Anstruther, the 62nd Regiment's personnel broadly reflected the British realm with an officer corps and soldiery comprised of equal numbers of English and Irishmen, some Scots, and even a French nobleman. Because volunteers were difficult to find due to the unpopularity of the American war, the British Ministry infused the regiment with over one hundred Germans recruited in George III's Electorate of Hanover, thereby substantially altering the regiment's personnel cohesion. Although the 62nd Regiment was deemed "but very indifferent" in May 1775, it nevertheless embarked for the relief of Canada less than a year later.[4]

While the regiment did not exemplify Britain's best, the arms and accoutrements it received before leaving Ireland in 1776 were

**62nd Regiment of Foot Cartridge Pouch**

*Troiani Collection*

This cartridge pouch, marked to the British 62nd Regiment of Foot, can hold a total of thirty-six cartridges in its wooden block: eighteen on top and eighteen underneath. Found in a Boston house in the 1800s, the pouch may have been taken from a soldier of the 62nd Regiment following the British surrender at Saratoga.

### New Hampshire Officer's Sword

*Courtesy of Brian and Barbara Hendelson*

This cuttoe belonged to Jeremiah Fogg, who served as paymaster of the 2nd New Hampshire Regiment during the Saratoga Campaign. Silversmith John Ward Gilman of Exeter, New Hampshire, made the hilt. A regimental muster roll lists Fogg as being on furlough (away from his regiment) in the weeks before the Battle of Freeman's Farm. It is unclear if he fought in the battle. Fogg was later promoted to the rank of captain.

top of the line. Their firelocks were the sleek Pattern 1769 Short Land muskets, the most advanced infantry firearms Ireland had to offer. The regiment's colonel replaced the men's old, worn cartridge pouches with Irish-made pieces of a new, technologically advanced pattern. The leather housing contained a removable wooden block that held eighteen cartridges on each side (thirty-six total) and could therefore carry twice the amount of ammunition of other, larger pouches.

Lacking expected shipments of new clothing, British regiments in Canada were instructed to trim their uniforms in the spring of 1777. Cocked hats were cut into horse-hair-crested caps, coats cropped into short-skirted jackets, and worn woolen breeches were replaced by linen ones cut from the army's stockpile of old tents. The 62nd Regiment procured locally manufactured pewter star-burst ornaments for their caps, which added a prideful embellishment to their docked

uniforms. Officers had similar changes made to their clothing in order to maintain a uniform appearance with their men.

The 62nd Regiment formed part of Lieutenant-General John Burgoyne's army during the Saratoga Campaign of 1777. The regiment was initially siphoned off to garrison Mount Independence, a captured stronghold of the American Revolutionaries overlooking Lake Champlain, where the men killed enough timber rattlesnakes (*Crotalus horridus*) to decorate

### New Hampshire Officer's Powder Horn

*Troiani Collection*

Micah Hoit, the owner of this 1775-dated powder horn, served as a lieutenant in the 2nd New Hampshire Regiment in 1777. The 2nd New Hampshire engaged in heavy fighting at the battles of Hubbardton (July 7), Freeman's Farm (September 19), and Bemus Heights (October 7). Since the two senior officers of his company were captured at Hubbardton, Hoit commanded the company at Freeman's Farm and Bemus Heights.

their leather bayonet scabbards with the skins. The regiment was later replaced by another British battalion and rejoined Burgoyne in time for the September 19 Battle of Freeman's Farm. Being the junior British regiment present, the 62nd formed the centerpiece of the British line and engaged American forces in one of the war's longest sustained land battles.

This scene shows the leftmost grand-division of the 62nd Regiment charging into the woods bordering Freeman's farm during an attempt to close in with the 3rd New Hampshire Regiment. Although trained in treeing—a fighting style formulated to combat adversaries in the woods—this was the first opportunity the regiment had to engage with the enemy using the tactic. The soldiers doffed their knapsacks, haversacks, and cooking kettles upon entering the farm field, which allowed them freedom of movement—something they found

useful as they ran after, and from, the Americans during the fight.

Shown here, Major Henry Harnage (bottom left foreground), seriously wounded in the abdomen from a shot through his side, is tended to by a drummer and his soldier-servant, Private John Pruit, while eighteen-year-old Lieutenant Gonville Bromhead looks back to his fallen commander. The regiment's senior lieutenant, Thomas Reynell (right midground, against a tree), lives his last moments after having been shot in the head. Later that day, his wife, Anne, who attended the army with their two young sons, learned of her husband's fate.

After about four hours of continual fighting, the battle ended in a tactical British victory but at great cost to the 62nd Regiment. Of the four hundred engaged, eleven commissioned officers were killed, captured, or wounded,

while the other ranks lost about fifty killed, one hundred wounded, and twenty captured. In the words of a fellow British officer, "That Corps suffer'd very much," more so than any other British regiment during the entire expedition.[5]

*Eric Schnitzer*

### Artist Comment

I visited the actual battlefield with renowned historian Eric Schnitzer, Park Ranger at Saratoga National Historical Park, to establish the scale and positioning of the figures. We posed people where both the British and Americans stood at approximately the same time of day and date so the lighting would be as it was on September 19, 1777. Very few Revolutionary War battlefields are as pristine as Saratoga and this afforded a rare opportunity to recreate the terrain exactly.

# 53rd Regiment of Foot Private, 1777

The 53rd Regiment's light infantry company surrendered at Saratoga on October 17. This light infantryman wears a distinctive leather cap and carries a hatchet in addition to the bayonet mounted on his musket. The 53rd Regiment was one of the few British regiments that had red-colored facings.

# SERGEANT, GRENADIER, ROYAL HIGHLAND EMIGRANTS 2ND BATTALION, 1777

THIS TWO-BATTALION UNIT OF LOYALISTS WAS raised in Boston, New York, Canada, and Novia Scotia mostly from Scottish veterans and emigrants. A small detachment of the Royal Highland Emigrants served in Burgoyne's army in 1777. The Royal Highland Emigrants were later designated the 84th Regiment of Foot.

# Morgan's Rifles

"I wish Colol Morgans Regt woud be spared to this department, I think we should then be in a Condition to see Genl Burgoyne with all his Infernals on any Ground they might choose."[6] Such were the words penned on July 27 by Major General Benedict Arnold in a letter to General George Washington during the darkest days of the Saratoga Campaign of 1777. Having abandoned forts, food, and war matériel, and suffered significant casualties in the July 7 Battle of Hubbardton, Vermont, the Northern Army faced its greatest crisis yet as it faced off against Lieutenant-General Burgoyne's superior British Army from Canada.

In America, rifles were endemic to Pennsylvania, Maryland, and the South, and while riflemen populated Washington's Main Army since the war's beginning, none had been added to the permanent establishment of the Northern Army. It was in June 1777 that Washington formed a new, provisional Continental Army rifle battalion, a Corps of Rangers, commanded by Colonel Daniel Morgan of the 11th Virginia Regiment. These light troops would be employed with ranging as well as flanking and harassing enemy forces.

The Detached Rifle Battalion was divided into eight subdivisions, five of which were comprised of officers and soldiers drawn from Virginia regiments and the remaining three from the Pennsylvania line. Men selected for the service were those "known to be perfectly skilled" with the use of rifles as well as "active and orderly in their behaviour."[7] Because the draftees were not all armed with rifles to begin with, Morgan was empowered to swap their smoothbore muskets with publicly owned rifles found in the hands of soldiers outside of his

**Pennsylvania Rifle**

*Courtesy of the Pennsylvania Society of Sons of the Revolution and its Color Guard*

During the Saratoga Campaign, the sharpshooting riflemen from Pennsylvania and Virginia under Colonel Daniel Morgan's command carried rifles like this Pennsylvania-made example. Moravian gunsmith Christian Oerter made this rifle in 1775. It features brass inlaid into its maple stock and Oerter's name engraved on its barrel.

new corps. He was also authorized to arrange for the exchange or purchase of rifles in private ownership.

Officers and soldiers alike were dressed in a variety of clothes, all of which reflected the uniformity or lack thereof in their parent regiments. Most common was the fringed linen hunting or rifle shirt, a garment that became as emblematic of riflemen as the rifles they wielded. Accoutrements included powder horns and bullet pouches; tomahawks and knives were commonly carried since very few rifles mounted bayonets. Rather than rely on bullets issued from the commissary of military stores, lead was delivered to the men so that they could cast balls matching the varying calibers of their rifles.

Ordered by Washington in mid-August to join the Northern Army, Morgan's Detached Rifle Battalion of four hundred officers and soldiers arrived by the end of the month and were placed in Arnold's Division. Command of the army's newly formed three-hundred-man Corps of Light Infantry was given to Morgan as well, creating in theory an elite combined-arms corps. However, with battle against the British close at hand, Morgan's troops had no time to train together or develop such tactics.

A late-morning skirmish in the woods a couple miles north of the American camp at Bemus Heights heralded the start of the September 19 Battle of Freeman's Farm. This scene depicts the Detached Rifle Battalion marching

to Freeman's farm early that afternoon, shortly after Arnold ordered Morgan forth to attack. The battalion, with Captain Van Swearingen's Pennsylvania company in the van, marches in a column of files as Morgan, wearing his white linen hunting shirt, urges them on. Behind Morgan is his second-in-command, Lieutenant Colonel Richard Butler of the 1st Pennsylvania Regiment, wearing the red cockade that marks him as a field officer. Morgan's blue-coated aide-major, Captain the Chevalier du Bouchet (a former French infantry officer who volunteered his services to the United States), watches with anticipation. Flanking the column is Captain Abraham Nimham's independent company of Stockbridge Indian volunteers, serving as scouts for the corps.

The resulting battle was a tactical British victory, albeit a Pyrrhic one. Although initially routed in the action, the riflemen were eventually re-formed and performed extraordinarily well in the fight, inflicting substantial casualties on the enemy while suffering four killed, eight wounded, and five captured. Morgan's riflemen proved to be the most invaluable troops of the Northern Army and were instrumental in winning the decisive October 7 Battle of Bemus Heights, after which the British Army from Canada was brought to heel at Saratoga on October 17, 1777.

*Eric Schnitzer*

### Artist Comment

Here again, being on the actual location was an immense help that cannot be overstated. The column snaking through the woods adds a lot of interest to the composition.

# A Soldier of the 8th Massachusetts Regiment, 1777

Commanded by Lieutenant Colonel John Brooks, the 8th Massachusetts Regiment fought at both Freeman's Farm and Bemus Heights. Many soldiers of the regiment wore linen hunting shirts issued for the campaign and carried newly imported French muskets. They participated in the attack on Breymann's Redoubt on October 7.

# BREYMANN'S REDOUBT, BATTLE OF SARATOGA, 1777

THE SARATOGA CAMPAIGN OF 1777 HAD ITS origins in the previous year's campaigning in northern New York. British forces under the command of General Guy Carleton, Military Governor of Canada, were unable to pursue a successful conclusion to their advance down the Lake Champlain–Hudson River corridor. On November 4, 1776, Carleton felt compelled to complete the evacuation of Crown Point and retreated back to Canada as winter had set in.

The British plans for 1777 called for a large army of over nine thousand troops under the command Lieutenant-General John Burgoyne to advance south from Canada along the Lake Champlain–Hudson River route to Albany, New York. A secondary, diversionary force under Lieutenant Colonel Barry St. Leger, composed mainly of Loyalists, British Indian Allies, and British soldiers totaling around 1,700, would move eastward roughly at the same time, from Lake Ontario down the Mohawk River and meet Burgoyne at or near Albany. The combined forces under Burgoyne would then come under the overall command of Lieutenant-General William Howe, Commander in Chief of British forces in America, and "open the communication to New York" for unspecified operations on the lower Hudson River Valley.[8] Contrary to a popular myth, Howe was never ordered north from New York City to physically meet Burgoyne and his army at Albany. As Lord Advocate Dundas, speaking before Parliament, stated: "That it was a plan of junction of co-operation, not a junction of the bodies of the armies."[9]

On May 6, 1777, the frigate *Apollo* dropped anchor off Quebec. Onboard was Lieutenant-General Burgoyne with orders, from Lord George Germain, to assume command of the British Army in Canada. On the last two days of May and the first days of June, Burgoyne's army began its expedition south toward Albany. During the advance it fought actions at Fort Ticonderoga and Mount Independence, Hubbardton, Fort Anne, and Bennington (Walloomsac, New York). The successful delaying efforts of Continental Army Major General Philip Schuyler and poor logistical planning and supply problems would plague Burgoyne's army throughout the campaign. In early September, Major General Horatio Gates having replaced Schuyler, ordered the Northern Army to retrace its steps and fortify Bemus Heights (near Stillwater, New York). On September 19,

**Brunswick Cartridge Box Plate**

*Troiani Collection*

Found near the Saratoga battlefields in the 1920s, this brass plate decorated the leather flap of a cartridge box carried by a Brunswick infantryman. The interlocking Cs stand for Carl I, Duke of Brunswick.

**Brunswick Officer's Gorget**

*Troiani Collection*

A Brunswick officer wore this large silver gorget with gilding and an enameled central device showing the white horse of the House of Hanover. One captured American officer described that the Brunswick officers "all wore Silver gorgets with the white Horse painted on a red ground in the center."[10] British officers also wore gorgets suspended around their necks as a sign of their rank and who they fought for.

1777, his forces halted the advance of Burgoyne's army in the fields around Freeman's Farm, an action known as the First Battle of Saratoga.

With Burgoyne's position becoming increasingly precarious, he set his army to work on a series of field fortifications and waited for Gates's reaction to British operations on the lower Hudson River Valley. Finally, on October 7, 1777, Burgoyne launched a reconnaissance-in-force of over 1,700 soldiers (made up of detachments from every corps) and ten artillery pieces against the left flank of the American fortifications.

They advanced southwest slightly less than a mile and deployed in a line of battle across two fields and woods near Barber's Farm. While in this position, the British force was attacked and driven back into the British Light Infantry Redoubt (also known as the Balcarres Redoubt) on the right flank of Burgoyne's fortified lines. Despite having been relieved of his command by Gates, Major General Benedict Arnold rode on to the field of battle. First against the center of Burgoyne's reconnaissance-in-force and then during the attacks on the Balcarres Redoubt, Arnold encouraged and led advance after advance with bravery and tactical leadership. After failing to breach the Balcarres Redoubt, he galloped north to join the American forces deploying to assault the other positions covering Burgoyne's fortified right flank. With elements of Brigadier General Ebenezer Learned's brigade, Arnold joined in the attack on two fortified cabins, which helped to cover the gap between the Balcarres Redoubt and the Breymann Redoubt. These cabins were undermanned and captured with relative ease.

As shown in this painting, the bulk of Learned's brigade and Colonel Daniel Morgan's light corps mounted an assault on the front of the Breymann Redoubt. Arnold joined the attack by storming into the rear and left flank of the position with part of Lieutenant Colonel John Brooks's Massachusetts Continentals and a collection of fifteen or twenty riflemen. A Brunswick grenadier platoon fired upon Arnold, killing his horse and wounding him in the leg. At about the same time large numbers of Americans poured over and through openings in the front of the fortification. As Colonel Heinrich Breymann was killed, resistance collapsed. With the fall of the Breymann Redoubt, almost all of Burgoyne's positions were exposed and became untenable. The Americans had won the Battle of Bemus Heights, also known as the Second Battle of Saratoga. By October 17, 1777, they had forced Burgoyne's army to surrender.

*Anthony Wayne Tommell*

# 4

# STALEMATE

Between 1778 and 1781, the Revolutionary War dragged on around British-occupied New York City.

Following the Battle of Monmouth in June 1778, few decisive battles occurred in the North. With the British Army centered in New York City, General Washington positioned the Continental Army nearby in the hills of New Jersey and the Hudson Highlands. The towns and farm fields in the no-man's-land between the two armies became bloody battlegrounds of a civil war. Revolutionaries and Loyalists fought each other for control. British, Hessian, and Continental troops foraged for supplies. The war also raged in Indian country, destroying native communities and pitting neighbor against neighbor. It appeared as if the Revolutionary War would not end.

The paintings in this chapter highlight the people who fought and died in those difficult years. One shows the woman known today as Molly Pitcher loading a cannon as the Battle of Monmouth rages on. Another shares the little-known story of the Stockbridge Indians. Others show the raw hand-to-hand combat of Revolutionary and Hessian dragoons and a raiding party of Loyalists and American Indians. The paintings convey the harsh reality of war.

# Molly Pitcher, Battle of Monmouth, 1778

IN HIS MEMOIR, CONTINENTAL ARMY VETERAN Joseph Plumb Martin included a description of the army's June 1778 departure from Valley Forge: "we left our winter cantonments, crossed the Schuylkill and encamped. . . . We had lain here but a few days, when we heard that the British army had left Philadelphia and were proceeding to New York, through the Jerseys. We marched immediately in pursuit."[1]

Martin's farewell to the log huts at Valley Forge was likely almost as pleasing to the then-seventeen-year-old private in the 8th Connecticut Regiment as was the prospect of bloodying British General Sir Henry Clinton's departing column. During the sixteen months before arriving at Valley Forge the prior December, Washington's army had been, with few exceptions, consistently and humiliatingly bested. From Brooklyn Heights to Germantown, they had escaped several near-fatal encounters. Few were unaware that many British officers continued to regard the rebels as ragamuffins and country clowns, such knowledge stoking the Continentals' smoldering desire for redemption and vengeance.

The army encountered more fuel for revenge after they crossed the Delaware into New Jersey. Such depredations as Private Martin now saw—"cattle killed and lying about the fields and pastures, . . . household furniture hacked and broken to pieces; wells filled up and . . . farmer's tools destroyed"—all of it compounded the Revolutionaries' animus toward their foes and refocused their thoughts upon the safety and welfare of distant families.[2] For many married soldiers, though, the family was no farther distant than the rear of their own column. Reflecting the mode of the time, the Continental Army community included numerous wives and children of the rank and file. In addition to serving as their husbands' helpmates, army wives also assisted with laundering, sewing, and caring for the sick and wounded, whether in camp or hospital. They typically received rations and pay for their work for the army.

There was probably little to distinguish Mary Hays from the many hundreds of other women scuffing up clouds of yellow dust from the New Jersey roads in 1778. Wife of William Hays of Proctor's Artillery Regiment, Mary was in her mid-twenties, common in appearance, but compact and strong. More than a decade of earning a wage through domestic service had conditioned her body to daily labor and her mind to the sense of responsibility expected of those who could be relied upon. When William enlisted in the spring of 1777, Mary was likely an ideal candidate to become an army wife.

By June 28, fifteen thousand Continentals and militiamen were concentrated around Englishtown; just five miles southeast, half of Clinton's twenty thousand–man column had already passed through Freehold, the seat of Monmouth County. The morning attack launched by the independently managed advance element of Washington's army against the extended column's center was greatly delayed, overly cautious, and poorly coordinated. Halted before many were even engaged, the men were astounded when ordered to withdraw. After the clearly beneficial infusion of professionalism and esprit gained from the Valley Forge training efforts, the sight of several hundred Americans in inexplicable retreat shocked and infuriated their comrades, none more than their commander in chief. Determined now to take direct control, Washington thundered to the front past a wide-eyed Private Martin: "After passing us, he rode on to the plain field and took observation of the advancing enemy; he remained there some time upon his old English charger, while the shot from the

British Artillery were rending up the earth all around him."[3]

Returning, General Washington "ordered the two Connecticut Brigades to make a stand at a fence, in order to keep the enemy in check while the Artillery and other troops" were brought up.[4] The ensuing hedgerow firefight developed into some of the most intense combat of the war. Greatly compounding risk to life, the heat at Monmouth was brutal. With the temperature nearing one hundred degrees, the overwhelming humidity and glaring sandy fields became unendurable. In not a few units of both armies, the heat killed more men than did enemy fire. After Washington brought forward a large body of Continentals to anchor an extended main line in rear of the hedgerow, five hundred picked men, including Private Martin, were skillfully moved undetected to the left flank. The 42nd Royal Highland Regiment, the renowned Black Watch, was attempting to use a nearby orchard as cover from which to launch a turning movement around the American left. Immediately upon discovery of this threat, several fieldpieces were rapidly moved to support the arriving picked New England infantrymen.

As this critical response team opened a heavy and well-coordinated fire on the high-landers, Martin saw something remarkable:

"A woman whose husband belonged to the Artillery, and who was attached to a piece in the engagement, attended with her husband at the piece the whole time; while in the act of reaching a cartridge and having one of her feet as far before the other as she could step, a cannon shot from the enemy passed directly between her legs without doing any other dam-age than carrying away all the lower part of her petticoat, —looking at it with apparent uncon-cern, she observed, that it was lucky it did not pass a little higher, for in that case it might have carried away something else, and continued her occupation."[5]

Thus, Mary Hays became Molly Pitcher. The traditional, and plausible, portrayal of events at Monmouth has Mary repeatedly tot-ing water, probably in a wooden bucket rather than a pitcher, to the gun crew until husband William fell under the weight of the heat or a wound. Illustrated in this painting, Hays stepped up to the vacant gunner position and apparently passed ammunition forward to the muzzle and may have also loaded and rammed the piece. Whatever her precise gunnery duties had been, word of her determination and tenacity apparently spread throughout the army in a matter of days as the Continentals celebrated their signal victory at Monmouth. Following William's discharge from service, the pair settled in Carlisle, Pennsylvania, where their only child, a son, was born about 1783. Widowed about five years thereafter, she remarried, becoming Mary Hays McCau-ley. In 1822, Pennsylvania's governor signed a legislative act awarding "Molly McColly" a quite generous lifetime pension, she being one of only three women granted pensions for services performed during the Revolutionary War. When she died at age seventy-nine in 1832, Carlisle's militia turned out to march in her funeral procession. Molly would have been proud.

*Bob McDonald*

# Battle of Kingsbridge (Stockbridge Indian Massacre)

Lieutenant Colonel John Graves Simcoe, commander of the Queen's Rangers, a Loyalist corps of cavalry and infantry formed in 1777, planned to launch an ambush on August 31, 1778. Then on duty near the modern border of the Bronx and Westchester County, New York, the Queen's Rangers and other Loyalist units, including the British Legion, had been skirmishing with Continental Army light infantry and patrols of Stockbridge Indians who served alongside the Continentals. Simcoe hoped to show the prowess of his corps and strike a blow that his enemy would not soon forget. What resulted that day was a bloody battle in no-man's-land, about three miles north of British-held Manhattan Island, that left about seventeen Native Americans dead and more seriously wounded.

Stockbridge Indians, named after their residence in Stockbridge, Massachusetts, began supporting and serving in the Continental Army in 1775. Stockbridge was a multiethnic native community that included Mahican, Housatonic, and Wappinger peoples from the Hudson Valley and western Massachusetts. English missionaries founded Stockbridge in the 1730s and worked to convert American Indians to Christianity. They also adopted some cultural practices and understandings from

the English colonists, blending them with their native traditions. Some Stockbridges fought alongside the New Englanders at the Battle of Bunker Hill and on September 1, 1775, Stockbridge leader Solomon Wa-haun-wan-wau-meet stated his support for the Continental Congress: "Depend upon it, we are true to you, and mean to join you. Wherever you go, we will be by your sides. Our bones shall lie with yours. We are determined never to be at peace with the red coats, while they are at variance with you."[6] In 1776, the Continental Congress authorized General George Washington to recruit Stockbridge Indians. During the Saratoga Campaign, Captain Abraham Nimham led a group of Stockbridge Indian volunteers to serve as scouts for Colonel Daniel Morgan's Detached Rifle Battalion. Individual Stockbridge Indians, such as Benjamin Waunechnauweet and Daniel Wauwaunpeguannant, served in Massachusetts and Connecticut regiments of the Continental Army in 1778. Some of them fought at the Battle of Monmouth. Later in the summer of 1778, a group of Stockbridges led by Daniel Nimham (father of Abraham Nimham) served with the Continental Army then stationed in White Plains, New York. The Stockbridges worked closely with Brigadier General Charles

Scott's corps of light infantry and dragoons to harass British, Hessian, and Loyalist troops who made incursions into Westchester County. Intelligence gathering was one of their primary duties. According to Hessian Jäger officer Captain Johann Ewald, the Stockbridges "constantly lay before our outposts and harassed them."[7]

On August 31, 1778, Colonel Mordecai Gist, under Brigadier General Scott's command, encountered a party of the enemy south of Philipse Manor Hall (which still stands in present-day Yonkers, New York) and exchanged fire, leaving one killed and taking three prisoners. That morning action precipitated further bloodshed later in the day. In the afternoon, about forty to sixty Stockbridges led by Daniel and Abraham Nimham and about forty Continentals under the command of Major John Steward pursued a party of green-coated hussars of the Queen's Rangers and fell into a trap laid by Lieutenant Colonel Simcoe. The pursuit led the Stockbridges into the full might of the hussars, along with cavalrymen of the British Legion led by Lieutenant Colonel Banastre Tarleton. The Loyalists clashed with the Stockbridges in the farm fields of brothers Frederick and Daniel DeVoe. According to Ewald, who saw the battlefield after the action, "hardly one of the Indians escaped with his life to tell what happened to his fellow warriors."[8] Brigadier General Scott wrote a letter to Washington at five thirty that evening to alert him of the devastation: "I am in Hopes it is not so bad as it at Preasant appears But I cant promise my self that it will be much Short of it."[9]

This painting shows the Stockbridge Indians in the midst of combat with the Queen's Rangers hussars. The houses of the DeVoe family are visible in the background. The hussars rode into the Stockbridges and slashed at them with long steel sabers. The Stockbridges fired their French muskets and swung them like clubs to knock the Loyalists off their horses, with some success. According to Simcoe, Trumpeter Arthur French of the Queen's Rangers swung his saber at a native soldier but missed and toppled off his horse (shown in the left foreground). As the Stockbridge Indian drew his knife, French pulled out his pocket pistol and shot the man in the head. Simcoe later recalled that "near forty of the Indians were desperately killed or wounded," including Daniel and Abraham Nimham.[10] In the "hot fight," according to Ewald, "The Indians as well as the American defended themselves like brave men against all sides where they were attacked. . . . No Indians, especially, received quarter, including their chief called Nimham and his son, save for a few."[11] Only two hussars were wounded, and one member of the British Legion was killed.

When Captain Ewald visited the bloodsoaked battlefield soon after the action, he took note of the clothing and equipment on the bodies of the slain Stockbridge Indians. Ewald wrote:

"Their costume was a shirt of coarse linen down to the knees, long trousers also of linen down to the feet, on which they wore shoes of deerskin, and the head was covered with a hat made of bast. Their weapons were a rifle or musket, a quiver with some twenty arrows, and a short battle-axe, which they know how to throw very skillfully. Through the nose and in the ears they wore rings, and on their heads only the hair of the crown remained standing in a circle the size of a dollar-piece, the remainder being shaved off bare."[12]

Ewald drew an accompanying sketch in his journal. The Stockbridge Indians' appearance reflected both Native American traditions and the fact that they had received arms from the Continental Army.

The defeat devastated the Stockbridge Indians who fought alongside the Continental Army. A smaller contingent continued to serve with Washington's army, under the leadership of Captain Hendrick Aupaumut, and received both pay and supplies for their duties. Today, in a park at the northern edge of the Bronx, a small stone marker commemorates the Stockbridge Indians who lost their lives on that same ground in 1778. The place is still referred to as Indian Field.

*Matthew Skic*

### Artist Comment

The photograph above shows a posing session for the Battle of Kingsbridge painting. The horses were posed first, followed by the models. I have only one reproduction of a Queen's Ranger green jacket and one hussar cap, so the models took turns being fully outfitted. The cap and jacket were made especially for this painting.

# RAIDERS OF THE MOHAWK VALLEY

Following the October 17, 1777, surrender of the British Army at Saratoga, New York, warfare in the northern theater changed dramatically. Gone were the days of large campaigning armies intent on permanent territorial conquest; instead, both sides engaged in numerous lighting-strike raids or large, sweeping military operations bent on obliteration.

By 1778, British ambassadorship to the "Northern Indians" was accomplished through three Indian departments. Superintendents and their agents dealt with trade, domestic concerns, and even influenced political and military affairs. One of these, the Six Nations Indian Department, made treaties with the Haudenosaunee, a league of six Iroquoian nations populating central and western New York—the Mohawk, Oneida, Onondaga, Cayuga, Seneca, and Tuscarora. But the war was tearing the centuries-old alliance apart; the Mohawk, Cayuga, Seneca, and most Onondaga sided firmly with the British, while the Oneida and most Tuscarora allied with the United States.

In 1778, the Six Nations Indian Department deputy superintendent, John Butler, as well as Joseph Brant (Thayendanegea) of the Mohawk Nation and other British-allied Haudenosaunee leaders, executed deadly raids against American backcountry settlements such as Cobleskill, New York (May 30), and Wyoming Valley, Pennsylvania (July 3). By September, one place targeted for attack was the Mohawk Valley settlement of German Flatts. So named because it was principally settled by German immigrants, German Flatts lay on opposite sides of the Mohawk River about eighty miles west of Albany. Two small forts—Fort Dayton north of the river and Fort Herkimer south of it—manned by Colonel Peter Bellinger's Tryon County Militia defended the community.

Operating out of Oghwage (present-day Windsor, New York), Loyalist Captain William Caldwell and Joseph Brant coordinated plans for their ninety-mile expedition. Caldwell's command included 200 officers and soldiers from Butler's Rangers, about 160 Six Nations Indian Department combatants (most of whom were Mohawks) and Loyalist recruits, and about 100 of Brant's Volunteers, most of whom were white American partisans "Clothed and painted Like Indians."[13] Apart from an easily dispersed nine-man scouting party sent by Bellinger, the marauders met no resistance and arrived near their target on September 16. After overnighting in seclusion during a torrential downpour, the war party struck at dawn.

The invaders sacked the settlements on both sides of the river, scorching, plundering, and killing as they went for nearly six hours, during which the paltry fort garrisons could do little more than watch. Sixty-three houses, fifty-seven barns, and four mills were destroyed, as was the community's plentiful harvest and a great number of hogs. The raiders took away an astonishing 235 horses, 229 milk and beef cattle, 269 sheep, and 69 oxen. Four civilians lost their lives, one of whom was burned in the fire that consumed his home. Nearly seven hundred people, over half of them children, were displaced; they survived only because they were forewarned the previous evening by John Helmer, one of Bellinger's nine scouts. Caldwell boasted that his strike force "would in all probability have killed most of the Inhabitants at the German flats" had the people not evacuated into the forts for safety.[14]

In this painting, the victorious raiders leave the burning remnants of German Flatts behind them. Mohawks and Loyalists alike carry off loot including alcohol, clothing, livestock, bags

of household valuables, and even a half-eaten loaf of bread. One warrior hoists a scalp high. Painted in black and vermillion, most of the Mohawks wear printed calico shirts and blue stroud matchcoats, blankets, or animal skins. Silver shirt-buckles and armbands bedeck their clothing while ear-wheels and bobs hang from slit earlobes, a cultural characteristic practiced by many Eastern Woodland Indian men. Butler's Rangers, dressed in green coatees with white facings, wear cartridge boxes around their waists that house eighteen rounds of prepared shot. Demonstrating wide-ranging cross-cultural influences, many Mohawks and Americans alike have powder horns and bullet bags, quillwork neck knife sheaths, woolen or leather leggings, and moccasins, and use tumplines to carry belongings on their backs. All carry tomahawks, knives, bayonets, swords, or wooden ball clubs, necessary weapons for melee-based combat. Two women, taken captive by a Mohawk war captain, contemplate their fate while Caldwell and the expedition's Indian Department commander, Captain Gilbert Tice, discuss their recent success.

*Eric Schnitzer*

### Artist Comment

In this painting, I tried to avoid the more idealized renderings of Native Americans in the eastern forests. After a two-hundred-mile trek through the woods to the Mohawk River Valley, every one of the raiders would have been ragged and filthy. Fully painted for war and among the greatest irregular fighters of any age, it was important to show the Native Americans as they really appeared on campaign. The photograph *(above)* shows three models taking a break from posing for the painting. I often change the colors and patterns of clothing in paintings to fit the scene.

# AMBUSH IN WESTCHESTER 1778

WESTCHESTER COUNTY, NEW YORK, WAS A war-ravaged no-man's-land in the fall of 1778, caught, as it was, directly between the Continental and British lines. Skirmishes played out daily in the roads. Hessians and lawless marauders terrorized the unhappy locals, pillaging homes and farms. Livestock, grain, and even clothing hung to dry was stolen in broad daylight. Many fled. To combat these depredations, Continental Army Brigadier General Charles Scott's corps of light infantry and dragoons patrolled the roads for bandits and attacked Hessians wherever they could.

Private Joseph Plumb Martin was seventeen years old when he was assigned to Colonel Richard Butler's light infantry regiment. "A motly group . . .," wrote Martin, "half New-Englanders and the remainder were chiefly Pennsylvanians,—two setts of people as opposite in manners and customs as light and darkness." Butler, a Pennsylvanian whom Martin described as a brave but "fiery austere hothead," relied on local supporters of the Revolutionary cause to guide him through Westchester's unmapped back roads and forests.[15] In late September, a trusted guide named Isaac Odell scouted a new location to

strike vulnerable Hessians—a defile on the Albany Post Road, just north of Peter Post's tavern in the present village of Hastings-on-Hudson. Butler and his guide set out with 250 men for the site at three o'clock on the morning of September 30. Major Henry Lee and two hundred dragoons in drab short coats trimmed in green were in the van. Their trumpeters, on white horses, wore uniforms with inverted colors. "We marched all night," wrote Martin. "Just at day-dawn we halted in a field and concealed ourselves in some bushes; we placed our sentinels near the road, lying down behind bushes, rocks and stoneheaps."[16]

A few miles down the road, a Hessian patrol led by Captain Karl Moritz von Donop was heading toward the Continental trap. The unsuspecting party of sixty Jäger on foot and twelve on horseback in sheepskin-padded saddles stopped Captain Johann Ewald, a fellow Jäger officer returning from an earlier patrol, near Peter Post's tavern. "I assured the good Donop that I had discovered no trace of the enemy," wrote Ewald, "but begged him to be careful to cover his rear and flanks, and to let only a few men go past the defile [ahead]."[17] Von Donop did not listen. He sent Lieutenant

Alexander Bickell with thirty foot-Jäger across the defile.

This painting shows the carnage that ensued because of von Donop's decision. Joseph Plumb Martin, likely describing Bickell's approach, wrote:

"When the front of them [the Hessians] had arrived "within hail," our Colonel rose up from his lurking place and very civilly coerced them to come to him. The party immediately halted. . . . [but their] commander seemed to hesitate. . . . Our Colonel then, in a voice like thunder, called out to him '*Come here, you rascal!*' but he paid very little attention to the Colonel's summons. . . . Upon which our Colonel ordered the whole regiment to rise from their ambush and fire upon them."[18]

Von Donop heard the firing. "He lost his presence of mind," wrote Ewald, "and sent Lieutenant [Balthasar] Mertz with his twelve horsemen past the defile to rush support to the foot Jägers."[19] When Mertz crossed the defile, Lee's dragoons charged from the woods. Shown here, they tore into Mertz's flank and rear. Isaac Dehaven, a Continental trumpeter, caught Mertz hurrying to draw his saber. The trumpeter slashed Mertz's face. Mertz fought back, but he soon surrendered. All but one of his twelve horsemen were hacked to pieces.

Bickell was cut off. He fled with his surviving foot-Jäger down a ravine to the Hudson River. Others ran into the hills. Von Donop took flight with what remained of his men. "I have never seen a battlefield on a small scale more horrible than the little spot on which this slaughter took place," wrote Ewald.[20] Butler suffered no losses and took eighteen prisoners. Brigadier General Scott paroled Mertz the next day with a letter of commendation for his valor.

Seventy years later, a historian interviewed eyewitnesses of the ambush. The witnesses said fighting took place along Edgar's Lane, the name used for that particular stretch of the Albany Post Road in the 1840s. The skirmish was thereafter anachronously known as the Battle of Edgar's Lane.

*David J. Jackowe*

### Artist Comment

Falling horses are always problematic to paint as it is difficult to recreate something that looks credible. In this case, I had photographed a horse stumbling at a jump and then changed the legs to exaggerate the tumble further. The actual location of this ambush is now totally paved over and built up, but the modern road still roughly follows the same path as the historic post road. In the background, the Hudson River and Palisades remain unchanged.

# HESSE-HANAU ARTILLERY DRUMMER 1781, PARADE DRESS

THIS DRUMMER OF AFRICAN DESCENT WEARS A white linen summer dress uniform and "turban" as a member of the Hesse-Hanau Artillery. Three Black men, who may have escaped from slavery in search of their freedom, served as drummers in the Hesse-Hanau Artillery. An officer of the artillery described the "turban" the drummers received and wore when on parade: "its crown is covered with crimson silk in the form of a bowl and tied in front with a ribbon . . . on the left side are two intermixed red and white feathers about six inches high."[21] Other Hessian and Brunswick regiments that served in America added drummers of African descent to their rolls. Some of those men traveled to Germany with their regiments following the war. A few postwar paintings of the regiments illustrate drummers of African descent wearing similar feather-decorated headwear.

# 5

# WAR IN THE SOUTH

FIGHTING IN THE CAROLINAS, GEORGIA, AND VIRGINIA FROM 1779 TO 1781 WORE OUT THE British Army.

Headquartered in New York City, British General Sir Henry Clinton planned for victory in the Revolutionary War by conquering the South. By first securing coastal cities such as Charleston, Savannah, and Wilmington, Clinton then expected weakness from the Revolutionaries and strength from the Loyalists in the countryside. But this southern strategy did not go according to plan.

Even with victories at Savannah (1779), Charleston (1780), and Camden (1780), fewer Loyalists turned out than expected. Revolutionary militias in the swamps and the mountains wreaked havoc on British troops and supply lines. Meanwhile, the small Southern Army, a department of the Continental Army, managed to live to fight another day against superior British forces.

The paintings of the Battle of Kings Mountain and the Battle of Guilford Courthouse in this chapter capture the successes of the Revolutionaries and the struggles of the British Army and Loyalists in the South.

# THE BATTLE OF KINGS MOUNTAIN, OCTOBER 7, 1780

By mid-1780, the situation of the Revolutionary cause in the Carolinas appeared quite bleak. Charleston had fallen to the British in May, resulting in the incarceration of more than five thousand Continental troops. Steps were now taken to crush all remaining rebel opposition in the Southern backcountry. Fast-moving British and Loyalist light corps were sent out on seek-and-destroy missions against the Continental, state, and militia forces that had heretofore eluded capture. The Revolutionary forces were scattered and in disarray, while the British standard was raised among the Loyalist sympathizers in that region. Major Patrick Ferguson, commander of the American Volunteers, was appointed the Inspector of Militia and ordered to "form into Corps all the young and unmarried Men of the Provinces of Georgia and the two Carolina's" into battalions or independent companies, as "Circumstances will admit."[1] By midsummer, Ferguson had already succeeded in organizing, training, and partially arming and equipping a number of battalions in South Carolina. Having routed a second Southern Army in August at the Battle of Camden and secured most of the major settlements in the South Carolina Piedmont, British Lieutenant-General Charles Cornwallis

contemplated an invasion of North Carolina. While the main army advanced north under his command toward Charlotte, Ferguson would lead a smaller, flanking force farther to the west, crushing all opposition from that quarter, a known hotbed of Revolutionary activity.

The backbone of Ferguson's column consisted of his American Volunteers, a detachment of picked men drawn from various Loyalist regiments from the north. Although they wore the different regimental coats of their parent corps, mostly red with blue or green facings and some in green coats, Ferguson did his best to instill a sense of group identity for the new corps by at least enforcing uniformity in the form of their cocked hats and in the method of wearing their hair. He had also succeeded in procuring short, British-made, muzzle-loading military rifles for half of his rangers, the others being armed with muskets and bayonets. He trained his men to fight in a loose, two-rank formation with the riflemen posted in the rear rank, protected by the bayonets of the musket men to their front, responding to his various commands by sound of whistle and waving of the hat. Ferguson himself carried the breech-loading rifle of his own invention that bore his name, as did a few of his other officers,

in addition to swords. Most of Ferguson's command, however, consisted of Loyalist militia—mostly men from the Ninety-Six District of South Carolina, trained (to some degree) by Ferguson to fight in a similar manner to his American Volunteers. They were armed with a mix of their own guns, mostly long rifles or fowling pieces, along with captured French muskets and bayonets. Needing a dependable cavalry force, Ferguson created a small cadre of rifle dragoons or mounted infantry from the American Volunteers and issued cutlasses to them and some of the mounted militia for fighting while on horseback.

With approximately one hundred of the American Volunteers and nearly one thousand militia, Ferguson marched toward the North Carolina border and issued a warning that threatened "fire and sword" to those who resisted British rule.[2] Various over-mountain leaders determined to gather a force together capable of eradicating Ferguson and his Loyalists once and for all. A rendezvous was set for September 25 at Sycamore Shoals, at which more than one thousand Revolutionary militia and volunteers from both sides of the Blue Ridge—Carolinians, Virginians, and Georgians—showed up. Setting out the next

day, they were joined by additional militia from the Carolinas over the course of more than a week's march, swelling their numbers to more than eighteen hundred men, mostly mounted riflemen. Learning of their advance, Ferguson began a slow retreat, after dispatching couriers to Cornwallis in which he brashly stated that reinforcements of "Three or four hundred good soldiers, part dragoons, would finish this business."[3] On October 6, Ferguson took post on the summit of Kings Mountain and awaited such troops, as well as the return of a two hundred-man scouting party that he had sent out that morning. Kings Mountain was a footprint-shaped ridge whose crest dominated the adjoining hills by no more than some sixty feet. Nearly treeless at the top, it had rocky slopes heavily wooded with old-growth hardwoods, an element that would contribute in no small part to his undoing.

That evening, the Revolutionaries divided their force, sending a fast-moving column of some nine hundred of the "best horsemen" ahead to close on their intended prey before it eluded them, "the weak horse and footmen to follow as fast as possible."[4] Riding all night in a heavy rain that dissipated to a drizzle by the following morning, the fast column linked up with other militia forces within seven miles of

Kings Mountain at about day. Ferguson's position was confirmed by locals and a strategy was devised on how to mount the attack. Advancing by two columns to the right and left, respectively, the riflemen encircled the perimeter of the mountain. By mid-afternoon, the weather had cleared and most of the regiments had reached their assigned positions before they were detected and an alarm sounded. After overrunning the Loyalist guard posts downslope, "they were able to advance in three divisions . . . to the crest of the hill in perfect safety until they took post and opened an irregular but destructive fire from behind trees and other cover."[5] Ferguson attempted to counter this by having the American Volunteers push them back by point of bayonet, the "mountaineers flying whenever there was danger of being charged by the bayonet, and returning again so soon as the . . . detachment faced about to repel another of their parties," according to Alexander Chesney, a Loyalist militia captain.[6] For nearly an hour, the battle raged in this seesaw fashion. Finally, the North Carolina Loyalist militia, after repulsing two attacks, ran out of ammunition and broke, throwing the rest of the militia into confusion, who began to crowd the flanks of the regulars. Ferguson, realizing that the situation was desperate, called for

another bayonet charge before rebel riflemen overran their position.

Shown at the center of this painting, Ferguson led a forlorn hope down the hill consisting of a handful of mounted men—two militia officers and the few dragoons of the American Volunteers yet alive—hoping to cut a swath through the advancing riflemen. Although he was dressed in a light-colored hunting shirt, locals had forewarned the attacking riflemen to be on the lookout for an officer dressed in this manner and wielding a sword in his left hand (his right incapacitated by an earlier war wound). Ferguson fell at Kings Mountain with at least seven lead balls in his body. With his death, further Loyalist resistance crumbled in the region. This crushing defeat of the Loyalists signaled the beginning of the end for British ascendancy in the Carolina backcountry.

*James L. Kochan*

### Artist Comment

Jim Kochan was kind enough to shoot the background pictures at the location on a date close to the battle anniversary and at the correct time of day. Due to a shortage of cavalry sabers, some of Ferguson's mounted contingent were equipped with British naval cutlasses.

# Trooper, Nelson's Virginia Corps of State Cavalry, 1780–1781

John Nelson, who initially served as a captain in the Continental Army's 1st Regiment of Light Dragoons, was appointed to be major commandant of the Virginia Corps of State Cavalry in 1779. He led the corps in support of the Continental Army in the Carolinas and Virginia in 1780 and 1781.

**Continental Army**
**"New Construction" Cartridge Box**
*Troiani Collection*

This cartridge box demonstrates an attempt by the Continental Congress to improve and standardize the equipment of the Continental Army. In 1777, Congress received repeated complaints from army officers about poor-quality cartridge boxes made of "miserable Materials" that did not protect ammunition from wet weather.[7] Congress approved a new design the following year made of thick leather with a large flap. Soldiers in the Continental Army began to receive these new construction cartridge boxes as early as 1779. They were made to imitate durable British Army cartridge boxes.

**British Cartridge Pouch**
*Troiani Collection*

British grenadiers and battalion troops usually carried cartridge pouches like this one that held twenty-nine rounds of ammunition in a wooden block. Light infantrymen typically carried smaller-capacity cartridge boxes. Made of stout leather with a buff leather strap, the pouches were heavy when full of lead musket balls and gunpowder. Their large flaps did well to keep foul weather from ruining the paper cartridges held inside.

**Canteen Marked USTATES**

*Museum of the American Revolution*

This rare wooden soldier's canteen is marked USTATES, indicating Continental Army usage. Alarmed by chronic shortfalls in arms and equipment caused in part by thefts and negligence, the Continental Congress directed in February 1777 that all the arms and accoutrements belonging to the country should be marked to show ownership by the United States.

**British Tin Canteen**

*Troiani Collection*

British soldiers received tin canteens, such as this example, as part of their standard equipment. Made of tin-coated sheet iron, it is relatively lightweight compared to a wooden canteen of the same period. The water carried in these canteens was essential to prevent dehydration on campaign.

**French Musket Marked UNITED:STATES**

*Troiani Collection*

This musket is one of over one hundred thousand French arms imported into the United States during the Revolutionary War. It is marked UNITED:STATES on the stock, evidence of its use by a soldier in the Continental Army. In 1777, Sergeant Jeremiah Greenman of Rhode Island noted that he and fellow soldiers encamped at Morristown, New Jersey, "were ordered to town to have our guns stamped US" according to a directive of the Continental Congress from earlier that year.[8]

**Pattern 1769 Short Land Musket**

*Troiani Collection*

This musket is one of about eight thousand muskets made in Ireland for use by regiments of the British Army's Irish establishment that fought in America during the Revolutionary War. Its barrel is engraved for the 57th Regiment of Foot, a regiment that shipped off from Cork, Ireland, in 1776. Armed with Short Land muskets, possibly including this example, the 57th Regiment's light infantry company served in Lieutenant-General Cornwallis's army in the South and surrendered at Yorktown in 1781.

# BATTLE OF GUILFORD COURTHOUSE

Almost exactly a month after Major General Nathanael Greene's Southern Army crossed the Dan River, just in front of the British advance guard, Greene positioned his army at a small crossroads called Guilford Courthouse. Lieutenant-General Charles Cornwallis's British took on the challenge, marching some twelve miles, the last six of which were literally a running skirmish, to engage the Americans.

After a very short artillery exchange, the British infantry advanced against North Carolina militia manning the first line beyond open fields. Although most of them fled after only one volley, the militia dealt out some punishment before withdrawing as planned. On the flanks, many militiamen stayed and fought alongside American flanking parties led by Colonel William Washington and Lieutenant Colonel Henry Lee.

As the British advanced into the dense woods beyond the first line, they brought all their infantry into an irregular battle line that moved as rapidly as the woods and American resistance permitted. When Virginians on the second line's northern flank advanced to meet them, the 23rd Regiment of Foot rolled them up, scattering them like "sheep frightened by dogs."[9] The remaining Virginians stood fast, bending but

not breaking, creating an L-shaped position as their right flank bent back onto the New Garden Road that served as the battlefield's axis.

After heavy fighting that Colonel Otho Holland Williams described as the loudest he heard during the war, the Virginians were forced to the rear. This retreat was brought about by having fired enough times to wear down their flints, foul their muskets, and by having suffered wounds inflicted by the British. The fighting was severe enough that Cornwallis was very nearly captured (being saved by Sergeant Roger Lamb of the 23rd Regiment) and Brigadier General Edward Stevens, commanding the Virginia militia south of the road was wounded. Cornwallis had two horses shot from underneath him during the intense fighting.

Because the different British regiments moved eastward at differing rates, they arrived at the third line individually, rather than as a solid mass. The first to arrive was the 33rd Regiment of Foot. Led on by Lieutenant Colonel James Webster, they went down a steep slope, crossed old fields and a vale bisected by a creek, and went after two American cannon. In doing so, they ran into an ambush as one Maryland and two Virginia regiments, backed by two 6-pounders, blasted them with volleys of buck and ball and

case shot. The 33rd Regiment withdrew, climbing the steep slope and lying down to avoid the hail of shot, now covered in a virtual redoubt protected by the terrain from any more damage.

At this time, the 2nd Battalion of Guards, a composite unit created by drafting men from all guards units in Britain, came to the western edge of the vale. Seeing two cannon amid the 2nd Maryland Regiment aligned on the opposite slope and angling east along the road, the guards went down into the vale and crossed the small creek. As they moved forward, the 2nd Maryland tried to swing its left companies, wheeling right to form a battle line facing the guards. There was a feeble effort to fire and charge, marked by orders that were countermanded. Confusion ensued due to few officers known to their men. When the guards slammed into them, the Marylanders broke. At the guns, a company of North Carolina Continentals sold their lives dearly trying to protect the cannon but were overrun, suffering numerous bayonet wounds in the process.

As the guards swarmed over the guns, the 1st Maryland Regiment, like the 2nd Battalion of Guards, a composite of eight early war regiments, began moving toward them, masked by a screen of trees in wet ground unsuitable for agriculture. Left flank guards began firing and the Maryland commander, Colonel John Gunby, went down under his horse. Lieutenant Colonel John Eager Howard led the Marylanders on, starting platoon firing when the two regiments were so close that the flames from musket barrels were recorded as overlapping.

Once firing began, the guards were preoccupied with the Marylanders and did not see Colonel William Washington's light dragoons (accompanied by both Virginia and North Carolina militia light horsemen) galloping toward them behind the trees, coming through open space north and west of the courthouse. As the guards concentrated on the Marylanders, the dragoons hit their right and rear with a smashing blow, knocking over men, sabering others, and rampaging through the guards. The fighting turned into a melee of hand-to-hand combat as Washington's men wheeled and rode through the fringes of fighting, and then turned to pursue those breaking away.

Washington was leading a party at the gallop toward a group of British officers he saw on a knoll overlooking the vale. His helmet fell to the ground and he dismounted to recover it as his troopers rode toward the British. At this point Cornwallis ordered his artillery to fire into the dragoons, mortally wounding Captain Griffin Fauntleroy, Washington's second-in-command, who now led the dragoons. In the background some case shot fell among the struggling 2nd Battalion of Guards and Marylanders.

Greene had already decided to break off the engagement, keeping his army intact for another fight. Pursuit was very limited, as the British had suffered devastating casualties to the officers and noncommissioned officers during the three hours of fighting. Roughly 28 percent of the British army were made casualties. Only 7 to 10 percent of Greene's army were wounded and killed, but if the missing militia are included in the figure, Greene lost over 30 percent of his men.

This painting shows Washington's light dragoons hitting the guards' right rear. What order had been restored after their successful charge was destroyed as the dragoons surprised the guards already occupied with trying to repel the Marylanders. This moment might be seen as the climatic instant of the Battle of Guilford Courthouse. Two of the finest regiments to fight in the Southern Theater, in some ways mirror images of each other, went at each other with unbridled ferocity.

The charge of Washington's light dragoons stands out as unusual in the heavily wooded plateau where the battle was fought. Except when Washington rode to the sound of battle, cavalry played almost no role around Guilford Courthouse. Their impact at this critical time and place is a classic example of mass and shifted momentum toward the Americans, who were able to disengage and survive to fight again.

*Lawrence E. Babits*

# 6

# YORKTOWN

GENERAL GEORGE WASHINGTON'S GREATEST MILITARY VICTORY CAME AT YORKTOWN, VIR-
ginia, in 1781.

Following a long march south from the Hudson Highlands, the allied American and
French forces under the respective commands of Washington and General Jean-Baptiste
Donatien de Vimeur, Comte de Rochambeau, prepared to besiege British Lieutenant-
General Charles Cornwallis's army at Yorktown. On October 9, Washington himself fired
the first American cannon. Hemmed in on both land and sea and bombarded by artillery
fire, Cornwallis's army surrendered on October 19. Washington's triumph at Yorktown
did not end the war, but it helped convince the British to seek peace. On September 3,
1783, the Treaty of Paris officially concluded the Revolutionary War. Independence for the
United States had been won and the Continental Army was disbanded.

The paintings in this chapter portray key moments from the victory at Yorktown, beginning with the Continental Army's march through Philadelphia on the way to Virginia. The
final painting, *The Veteran's Return*, takes us to the war's end in 1783 and shows a Continental Army soldier arriving back at home. Many veterans struggled with poverty in their postwar lives after years of dealing with meager provisions and a lack of pay. Veterans who had
been enlisted men in the army waited for decades for the federal government to authorize
pensions for their relief.

# Brave Men as Ever Fought

On February 23, 1831, African American abolitionist and Philadelphian James Forten, then sixty-four years old, penned a letter to his friend and fellow abolitionist William Lloyd Garrison. Forten reflected upon a moment in his home city from nearly fifty years earlier, a warm and memorable September day in 1781. "I well remember," Forten wrote, "that when the New England Regiment passed through this city on their way to attack the English Army under the command of Lord Cornwallis, there was several Companies of Coloured People, as brave Men as ever fought."[1]

In this painting, James Forten looks on as the Continental Army marches west through Philadelphia by way of Chestnut Street on September 2, 1781, Forten's fifteenth birthday. The young sailor, who had recently returned to port following his first voyage aboard the American privateer ship *Royal Louis*, joined fellow city residents lining the streets and peering out of house windows to catch a glimpse of the thousands of soldiers marching in a long column of platoons. The troops kicked up clouds of dust as they marched "in slow and solemn step" past Carpenters' Hall and the Pennsylvania State House (now known as Independence Hall), the brick facade of which is visible in the background.

Army surgeon James Thacher later recalled that "we raised a dust like a smothering snow-storm."[2]

The Rhode Island Regiment, shown here, is the New England Regiment with "several Companies of Coloured People" that Forten referred to in his 1831 letter. Two of the regiment's nine companies (about sixty-five privates each) were entirely made up of Black and Native American private soldiers led by white officers. The racial segregation by company in the Rhode Island Regiment was a rare practice in the Continental Army. Most men of color in other regiments of the army served in integrated companies, standing shoulder to shoulder with white private soldiers. The Rhode Island Regiment was formed in 1781 following the merger of the state's two Continental Army regiments. The 1st Rhode Island Regiment had been raised in 1778 as a unit composed entirely of private soldiers of African and Native American ancestry led by white officers, the only time such a regiment was formed in the Continental Army. The soldiers of the Rhode Island Regiment included many formerly enslaved men who were declared "absolutely free" upon their enlistment in 1778.[3]

As part of their uniform, the soldiers of the Rhode Island Regiment received black leather caps painted with a white anchor, the state symbol of Rhode Island. The regiment was also issued linen hunting shirts and overalls in May and June of 1781. A small watercolor sketch by French officer Lieutenant Jean-Baptiste-Antoine de Verger, painted after the Siege of Yorktown, shows a Black soldier of the Rhode Island Regiment wearing overalls and an anchor-decorated cap adorned with blue and white feathers.

Philadelphia marked the midpoint and, as the home of the Continental Congress, the most symbolic stop of the march to Yorktown by these Rhode Islanders and thousands of other Continental troops. An expeditionary force of about five thousand French troops led by General Jean-Baptiste Donatien de Vimeur, Comte de Rochambeau, joined them on the journey. Just over a month after marching past the Pennsylvania State House where the Declaration of Independence had been adopted in 1776, the allied armies forced an army under the command of British Lieutenant-General Charles Cornwallis to surrender. The Siege of Yorktown was one of the grandest victories for the Revolutionary cause.

In his letter to William Lloyd Garrison from nearly fifty years later, James Forten included the anecdote about the "brave men" of color in the Continental Army before their triumph at

Yorktown to prove a point. Forten disagreed with the rising American colonization movement in the 1820s and 1830s, which sought to remove African Americans from the United States and resettle them in Africa. He instead supported educational opportunities for people of color. Forten argued that African Americans "are contented in the land that gave us birth, and which many of us have fought for."[4] His own wartime service on a privateer ship and the soldiers of the Rhode Island Regiment shaped Forten's opinions. He suspected that "all this appears to be forgotten now" by younger generations of Americans.[5] Rather than be forgotten, Forten hoped that Black veterans would be honored as Revolutionaries who forged a nation founded on promises of liberty and equality. He believed that those men and their descendants deserved to enjoy the full rights of citizenship in the United States. Future generations of Americans embraced Forten's more inclusive vision.

*Matthew Skic*

### Artist Comment

The models who posed for the Rhode Islanders came from all over the Northeast and did a great job being very patient with my persnickety posing sessions. To start the work itself, I did a pencil drawing on the canvas *(top)* and then I painted the entire scene with brown tones. This is tedious, but I like to solve problems on detailed paintings before the real painting starts. When I add a burnt sienna wash over the entire canvas *(center)*, a traditional technique, it gives the work a uniting tone and inner glow. I then like to rough the entire painting in *(bottom)* and bring up the details, much like a blurry photograph coming into focus. The building had to be completely painted in first before all the guns with bayonets could be done.

# The Battle of the Hook, 1781

In the early morning hours of October 3, 1781, a column of empty wagons lumbered out from behind British fortifications at Gloucester Point, across the York River from Yorktown, Virginia. Alongside rode approximately 150 mounted troopers of Lieutenant Colonel Banastre Tarleton's British Legion, 100 horsemen of Lieutenant Colonel John Graves Simcoe's Queen's Rangers, a few mounted Hessian Jäger under Captain Johann Ewald, and 40 mounted grenadiers from the 23rd Regiment of Foot under Captain Forbes Champagne. An infantry detachment of some 60 rangers and Jäger put the British total that morning at close to 300 mounted troops and 60 infantrymen.

Aware of Tarleton's foraging expedition, Franco-American forces under French Brigadier General Gabriel de Choisy, with Brigadier General George Weedon commanding the Virginia militia, set out at seven o'clock in the morning from Gloucester Courthouse thirteen miles to the north. Advancing on York River Road, the column was headed by Lauzun's Legion. The legion consisted of 150 infantrymen, 150 artillerists, and two squadrons of 150 hussars each, light cavalrymen wearing jackets decorated with elaborate trimmings of braid and cylindrical caps, whose colored cloth hanging from the top was attached to the right shoulder to defend against saber cuts. Their uniform, mustaches, and braids of hair on either side of the face symbolized the Eastern European origins of the hussar tradition. At their head rode Armand Louis de Gontaut, Duc de Lauzun, followed by thirty-five men of the First Squadron who were armed with lances. Also riding with the advance guard were some 30 horsemen of Lieutenant Colonel John Webb's Virginia Volunteer Cavalry. Behind them rode the remainder of the First Squadron followed by the Second Squadron of Hussars under Lieutenant Colonel Robert Dillon, and the 160 men of the Regiment of Virginia Grenadiers under Lieutenant Colonel John Mercer.

Shortly after ten o'clock in the morning, with the loaded forage wagons on their way back to Gloucester Point, Tarleton learned of the allied column behind him and decided to offer battle at a site about two miles north of Gloucester Point. When hussar and Virginia cavalry scouts made contact with a detachment of Jäger and Queen's Rangers infantry posted in ambush along the road, Lauzun, hearing the carbine and musket fire and anxious for a fight, advanced at a gallop.

Tarleton was waiting for Lauzun in an open field with cavalry arrayed in his rear.

Ostensibly challenging Lauzun to a duel, Tarleton advanced with a small detachment of his British Legion. According to Lauzun, "Tarleton picked me out, came to me with his pistol raised." Like the knights of old, "we were going to fight between our respective troops." The hussars, however, had followed their colonel in his headlong gallop, and Tarleton's dragoon guard rushed the field to support their leader. Tarleton's "horse was thrown down by one of his dragoons who was being pursued by one of my lancers," Lauzun reported.[6] Tarleton had gone down with his horse, causing the whole British cavalry to gallop across the field to protect its commanding officer. But in their headlong rush to rescue Tarleton, his cavalry lost all unit cohesion and was unable to carry the attack to the vastly outnumbered Lauzun, who retreated behind Dillon's hussar squadron, which had just reached the battlefield.

As illustrated in this painting, the launch of a counterattack by the now three-hundred-strong allied French and American cavalry made the Battle of the Hook the largest cavalry engagement of the Revolutionary War. The hussars pushed back Tarleton, who responded by ordering about sixty men from the 17th Light Dragoons and the 23rd Regiment to dismount

and reinforce his infantry line. The British
infantry advanced under cover of the woods,
forcing the hussars to retreat. At this critical
juncture, Mercer's grenadiers reached the battlefield, forcing the outnumbered Tarleton to
call a final retreat to his earthworks at Gloucester Point where he stayed for the remainder
of the Siege of Yorktown. Sixteen days later,
Cornwallis's army surrendered.

*Robert A. Selig*

### Artist Comment

I had only one complete and superbly crafted
Lauzun Hussar uniform to work with, so the
pool of models had to perfectly fit the clothing.
Eventually, enough suitably sized volunteers
were rounded up. The brave Armand Louis de
Gontaut, Duc de Lauzun, (on the white horse)
had the misfortune to be guillotined during the
French Revolution.

# Artillery of Independence, Siege of Yorktown, Virginia, October 9, 1781

THE ANNUS MIRABILIS, THE YEAR OF MIRACLES, WAS about to reach its grand finale when General George Washington's aides informed him in the early afternoon of October 9, 1781, that the time had come to open the American artillery on General Cornwallis's army. On September 14, eight weeks after he had left Phillipsburg on August 18, Washington had entered Williamsburg to the acclaim of some two thousand Continental Army forces and an equal number of Virginia militia under the Marquis de Lafayette and that of about three thousand French forces under the Marquis de St. Simon, who had arrived from the West Indies on the fleet of Admiral François Joseph Paul, Comte de Grasse, on August 29.

An allied force of 9,000 American and 8,500 French troops had assembled in Williamsburg by September 26. Though they were still waiting for the siege artillery to be debarked, since most of the American gun carriages sat marooned on the sloop *Nancy* on a sandbank in the James River, the allies set out for Yorktown on September 28. Until "the 6th. of October," Washington recorded, "nothing occurred of Importance—much deligence was used in debarking, & transporting the Stores—Cannon &ca. from Trebells Landing."[7]

On October 2, the first of the sixty pieces of Colonel John Lamb's 2nd Continental Artillery arrived outside Yorktown. On October 6, the oxen of the recently arrived American wagon train began to pull the first guns of the siege artillery into their emplacements. Finally, in the late afternoon of October 9, a windy day with overcast skies and temperatures in the mid-fifties, the Continental standard was hoisted over the Grand American Battery on the far right of the trenches closest to the York River. With French guns on the left of the siege line already firing, an anonymous soldier from Pennsylvania recorded that "American & French flags twisted on our batteries."[8] Continental Army surgeon James Thacher remembered "his Excellency General Washington put the match to the first gun."[9]

Shown in this painting under the watchful eyes of Brigadier General Henry Knox, the Marquis de Lafayette, and Baron Steuben, and accompanied by the cheers of his military family and of Continental troops, Washington put the wick to the touchhole of an 18-pounder, which discharge gave the signal for "a furious discharge of cannon and mortars," as Thacher reported gleefully. "Earl Cornwallis has received his first salutation," Thacher added.[10]

The artillery had a "good effect," Washington commented, since it "compelled the Enemy to withdraw from their ambrazures the Pieces which had previously kept up a constant firing."[11] Less than twenty-four hours later, most of Cornwallis's 244 pieces of artillery had been silenced. The allied artillery barrage from 155 pieces, including 18 howitzers and 30 mortars, continued almost unabated for the next eleven days. Thacher recollected mortar shells crossing the lines "like fiery meteors with blazing tails, most beautifully brilliant."[12]

With allied artillery pounding his defenses, Cornwallis had few options left. During the roughly 195 hours of artillery fire between three o'clock in the afternoon on October 9 and late in the afternoon of October 17, when Cornwallis agreed to a cease-fire on Washington's terms, allied batteries fired almost 15,500 shells of all calibers into Yorktown, some 80 rounds per hour. Two days later Cornwallis's defeated army laid down its arms. The artillery had won its work. The miracle no one had dared to hope for during the dark days of January 1781 at Morristown, New Jersey, had been achieved.

*Robert A. Selig*

## Artist Comment

I was fortunate to discover in the National Archives in Washington the shipping manifests for all the Continental Army artillery and equipage sent to Yorktown. This enabled me to paint the right type of gun carriages and other details for the scene.

### Continental Army Sergeant's Epaulettes

*Museum of the American Revolution, Gift of James B. Richardson III*

Sergeant James Davenport served in the Marquis de Lafayette's Corps of Light Infantry at the Siege of Yorktown. This pair of epaulettes marked him as a noncommissioned officer. The epaulettes may have been given to Davenport by Lafayette, who presented each corporal and sergeant in the Corps of Light Infantry with "an elegant sword, feather, two bobs [i.e., epaulettes], and as much silver lace as would lace the front of their caps."[13]

# French Grenadiers, Gâtinois Regiment, Yorktown, 1781

Wearing red epaulettes on their shoulders and red pompons on their hats, the grenadiers of the Gâtinois Regiment participated in the daring nighttime assault on Redoubt No. 9 during the Siege of Yorktown. A New York soldier recalled that the grenadiers hurled sacks of grenades (powder-filled iron shells) as they advanced. According to French Army uniform regulations adopted in 1779, the Gâtinois Regiment wore white coats with violet lapels.

# VICTORY AT YORKTOWN

SHORTLY AFTER TEN O'CLOCK ON THE MORNING of October 19, 1781, Colonel Elias Dayton of the 2nd New Jersey Regiment wrote the following words to his nineteen-year-old son Elias: "The drums are now beginning to beet for parade. I must now break off and hast to receive, a haughty cruel, unjust but now crest fallen foe."[14] By noon that day at Yorktown, Virginia, the approximately 5,800 troops that made up George Washington's Continental Army lined up on the east side of the road to Hampton. Behind them stood a little over 3,000 Virginia militiamen. Facing them across the road stood their French allies, some 400 officers and 4,000 men commanded by General Jean-Baptiste Donatien de Vimeur, Comte de Rochambeau, who had joined Washington's army on the journey to Yorktown in the summer of 1781. Another 225 officers and 3,300 men under General Claude-Anne de Rouvray, Marquis de St. Simon Montbléru, who had sailed in August 1781 from St. Domingue to Virginia on the vessels of Admiral François Joseph Paul, Comte de Grasse, stood in line with Rochambeau's troops. The Franco-American allies waited to receive the surrender of British Lieutenant-General Charles Cornwallis's army.

The third article of the instrument of surrender stipulated that the ceremony was to begin at precisely two o'clock in the afternoon, but it was closer to three o'clock when the British garrison began to "march out to a place . . . appointed in front of the posts . . . with Shouldered Arms, Colors cased and Drums beating a British or German March."[15] Cornwallis, commanding officer of British forces, had surrendered 462 officers, 6,602 rank and file, 840 naval personnel, and 177 other personnel, including 80 camp followers. Since Lieutenant-General Cornwallis pleaded sickness, the 5,500 officers and men that filed out of Yorktown on that cool autumn afternoon—around 1,500 sick and wounded remained behind in Yorktown and 900 troops surrendered later that afternoon across the York River in Gloucester—were led by Brigadier-General Charles O'Hara. Their dress reflected the global nature of the war. Red-coated English, Scottish, and Welsh regiments, looking splendid in the new uniforms that Cornwallis had distributed to keep them from falling into American hands, marched along with their Hessian and Ansbach auxiliaries in blue coats and American Loyalists. They filed past ragged but victorious Continentals, their officers in dark blue coats with buff

facings, their French allies dressed in white, with hussars on horseback in sky-blue dolmans, busby on their heads, and German-speakers of the Royal Deux-Ponts Regiment wearing coats dyed in the Wittelsbach Blue of the House of Zweibrücken.

As British drummers were beating any number of tunes "as if they did not care how," the faces of the defeated troops reflected, in the words of a British officer, a "mortification and unfeigned sorrow" that "will never fade from my memory."[16] A considerable number of them appeared to be "in liquor," as reported in *The Pennsylvania Packet* of November 13.[17] Some of the surrendering soldiers were angry enough to try and smash their flintlocks as they stacked them. To forestall even the thought of malevolence, Rochambeau had posted a few pieces of campaign artillery along the route to the surrender field. The mere presence of the French crews in their dark-blue uniforms sent a stern warning to the vanquished troops.

Once the 800-man Brigade of Guards had grounded its arms and was on its march back to Yorktown, the 150 soldiers of the 17th Regiment of Foot entered the field, followed by Captain Charles Anthorpe, who commanded the roughly 140 survivors of the 23rd Regiment

of Foot, shown in this painting. Captain Anthorpe may even have been joined by a bull-dog following the call to surrender. Sergeant Joseph Plumb Martin of the Continental Army's Corps of Sappers and Miners remembered a large British bulldog that frequently chased after the cannonballs fired toward American trenches. "Our officers wished to catch him . . . but he looked too formidable for any of us to encounter."[18]

At Yorktown, the Franco-American alliance won an important victory. But contemporaries did not consider it the end of the war. Writing on October 20, Washington thought Cornwallis's surrender but "an interesting event that may be productive of much good if properly improved."[19] In a letter to Robert Morris on October 26, Brigadier General Anthony Wayne described the victory as "an event of the utmost consequence & if properly Improved, may be productive of a Glorious & happy peace."[20] That peace came two years later, on September 3, 1783, when King George III "acknowl-edge[d] the said United States . . . to be free sovereign and independent states" through the Treaty of Paris.

*Robert A. Selig*

### Artist Comment

The models for the British Army were all posed in groups of three to five. Having enough uniforms and equipage in my prop department paid off, as this method allowed me to see how the shadows fell across one soldier to the next. Posing large groups in a fully sunlit scene made it easier than trying to get posing right one figure at a time. Some dog breeders have bred English bulldogs back to their eighteenth-century appearance, larger with longer legs and snouts. I luckily found a bulldog in the area to pose for me!

**Map of the Siege of Yorktown**

*Museum of the American Revolution, Gift of the Landenberger Family Foundation (founded by Bill Landenberger) and The Acorn Foundation Fund for History in Memory of Alexander Orr Vietor (David B. Vietor, Richard R. Vietor, Louise V. Oliver, Pauline V. Sheehan, Alexander W. Vietor, and Martha V. Glass, trustees)*

This map, engraved and published in Philadelphia in 1782, celebrates the triumph of the allied Continental and French forces over the British Army at the Siege of Yorktown in 1781. German-born Major Sebastian Bauman of the Continental Artillery served at the siege and created this map from his surveys of the battlefield taken three days after the British surrender.

# THE VETERAN'S RETURN

IN 1783, AT THE END OF THE REVOLUTIONARY War, the Continental Army discharged its soldiers and disbanded. Soldiers who shared tents, cooked together, and battled the British Army year-after-year parted ways. Joseph Plumb Martin, a soldier from Connecticut who served for seven straight years of the war, left the army like most of his comrades, with little more than his worn-out uniform and his signed paper discharge. Martin later reflected upon his abrupt departure from the army: "When the country had drained the last drop of service it could screw out of the poor soldiers, they were turned adrift like old worn-out horses, and nothing said about land to pasture them upon."[21] Acquiring land, promised by the Continental Congress as a reward for enlistment, was only one concern for veterans. Would they receive back pay owed to them? Would the paper currency or promissory notes they had in their pockets retain their value, or would they be considered worthless? Would there be employment opportunities back home?

This painting captures the moment of arrival for a Continental Army veteran who has returned to his New England home. Three generations of his family greet him with excitement and elation. The veteran is wearing the blue coat faced with red issued to him late in the war. His knapsack is filled with his meager belongings and has a blanket tied on top. He retained his wooden canteen, but the former soldier is without his musket, bayonet, and cartridge box. Most of the Continental Army's weapons and accoutrements remained government property after the war, and, while Congress granted some men their weapons and accoutrements as partial compensation for their service, some penniless veterans were forced to sell these items before they reached home. Veterans like the man shown in the painting approached the postwar period in different ways. Perhaps this soldier regaled his children with stories of serving under General Washington. Perhaps he did not want to recall the difficulties of war. Some men were proud of their service. Others remained disgruntled about the constant sufferings they endured in the army. Many hoped that the republic they fought to create would live up to its promise that all men are created equal.

Scenes like this were fleeting moments for veterans and their families. According to Joseph Plumb Martin, whose memoir was published in 1830, "many of the poor men who had spent their youthful, and consequently their best, days in the hard service of their country" battled poverty.[22] Referring to veterans, Martin added, "starved, ragged, and meager, not a cent to help themselves with, and no means or method in view to alleviate their condition. This was appalling in the extreme. All that they could do was to make a virtue of necessity and face the threatening evils with the same resolution and fortitude that they had for so long a time faced the enemy in the field."[23] Martin himself headed for what is now the state of Maine to settle on land he believed was owed to him. He started a family and served in politics, but he struggled to make ends meet and repay debts he accrued.

Continental Army officers received pensions from the United States, but it was not until 1818 (thirty-five years following the war's conclusion) that Congress passed the first Revolutionary War veterans' pension legislation to benefit men who had been common soldiers. Many of the soldiers who could have received pensions according to this legislation died in those intervening decades between 1783 and 1818. Veterans still alive in 1818 were eligible if they had served at least nine months "in the Land and Naval service of the United States" and were in "reduced circumstances."[24] Therefore, veterans of the militia, men who

served only short term, and those who were not struggling with poverty were excluded from receiving support with this act. So many men applied, about twenty thousand by November 1818, that Congress added a requirement in 1820 that pensioners had to reapply and prove their poverty. Applications revealed that thousands of former soldiers were destitute. Martin described himself as "a Labourer but by reason of age and infirmity I am unable to work—my wife is sickly and rheumatic."[25] Historian John P. Resch calculated that "about 20,000 veterans took the pauper's oath and submitted to the means test; and all but 2,000 got the benefit."[26] Later legislation would expand pensions to former militiamen and to widows of veterans. For thousands of former soldiers, a pension meant survival. Some thought it was too little, too late. In 1818, a commentator in Boston's *Niles' Weekly Register* wrote, "A little while, and no one will remain to *tell* the story of the revolution."[27]

*Matthew Skic*

## Artist Comment

This is a painting I always wanted to do, a Continental Army veteran returning to his humble home after years of hard service. The small New England house shown here dates from the late seventeenth century and is typical of a family farm of the era. The models who posed were newlyweds, so the emotions did not have to be forced, true love!

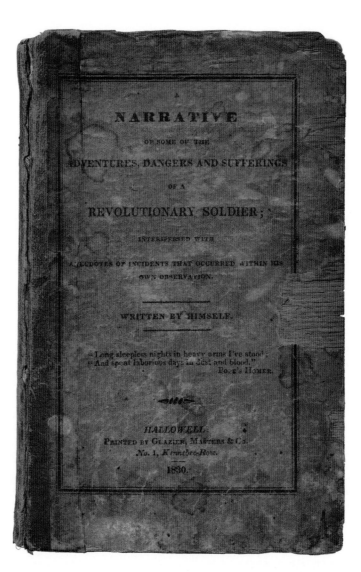

**Continental Soldier's Memoir**
*Museum of the American Revolution*
Anonymously published in 1830, Continental Army veteran Joseph Plumb Martin wrote this memoir of his seven years of military service. *A Narrative of Some of the Adventures, Dangers and Sufferings of a Revolutionary Soldier* recounted detailed stories of fighting at Monmouth and Yorktown, starvation at Morristown, and the various people, good and bad, he encountered. Martin concluded his memoir with a chapter describing the "ungenerous treatment" of Continental Army veterans, many of whom struggled with poverty, by the country they fought to create.[28] Today, Martin's memoir provides a valuable glimpse into the daily life and struggles of a common soldier.

# NOTES

## Chapter 1

1    John Adams, "Adams's Argument for the Defense," December 3–4, 1770, *Founders Online*, National Archives, https://founders.archives.gov/documents/Adams/05-03-02-0001-0004-0016.

2    Quote from John Munroe's deposition about the action at Lexington, see Elias Phinney, *History of the Battle at Lexington on the Morning of the 19th April, 1775* (Boston, MA: Phelps and Farnham, 1825), 35; For more on what Major John Pitcairn said at Lexington on April 19, 1775, see Jeremy Lister, *Concord Fight* (Cambridge, MA: Harvard University Press, 1931), 24.

3    John Pitcairn to Thomas Gage, April 26, 1775, quoted in David Hackett Fischer, *Paul Revere's Ride* (New York: Oxford University Press, 1994), 194.

4    Quote from an April 25, 1775 deposition written by participants in the fight at Lexington, see Abraham Tomlinson, ed., *The Military Journals of Two Private Soldiers, 1758–1775, with Numerous Illustrative Notes to Which Is Added a Supplement, Containing Official Papers on the Skirmishes at Lexington and Concord* (Poughkeepsie, NY: Abraham Tomlinson, 1855), 102.

5    Quote taken from Thomas Thorp's deposition about the action at Concord, see Josiah Adams, *An Address Delivered at Acton, July 21, 1835, Being the First Centennial Anniversary of the Organization of that Town* (Boston, MA: J.T. Buckingham, 1835), 43.

6    Hosmer is quoted in Fischer, *Paul Revere's Ride,* 209 and note 27.

7    Walter Laurie to Thomas Gage, April 26, 1775, see Allen French, *General Gage's Informers* (Ann Arbor, MI: The University of Michigan Press, 1932), 95–98.

8    Buttrick is quoted in Fischer, *Paul Revere's Ride,* 213.

9    Major-General Burgoyne's description of the Battle of Bunker Hill is from a letter he wrote to Lord Stanley on June 25, 1775, that was published in *The Pennsylvania Evening Post* (Philadelphia, PA) on November 16, 1775.

10   Quoted in Richard M. Ketchum, *Decisive Day: The Battle for Bunker Hill* (New York: Henry Holt and Company, 1999), 94.

11   Quoted in Ketchum, *Decisive Day,* 75.

12   Quote from a letter written by Lieutenant William Feilding on July 18, 1775, see Marion Balderson and David Syrett, eds., *The Lost War: Letters from British Officers during the American Revolution* (New York: Horizon Press, 1975), 33.

13   John Waller to unidentified (copy), June 21, 1775, Massachusetts Historical Society.

14   William Howe to Thomas Gage, June 21, 1775, Thomas Gage Papers, William L. Clements Library, The University of Michigan.

15   John Waller to unidentified (copy), June 21, 1775, Massachusetts Historical Society.

16   Martin Hunter, *The Journal of Gen. Sir Martin Hunter G.C.M.G., G.C.H.,* eds. Anne Hunter, Miss Bell, and James Hunter (Edinburgh, UK: The Edinburgh Press, 1894), 11.

17   John Waller to unidentified (copy), June 21, 1775, Massachusetts Historical Society.

18   John Waller to unidentified (copy), June 21, 1775, Massachusetts Historical Society.

19   John Waller to unidentified (copy), June 21, 1775, Massachusetts Historical Society.

20  Major-General Howe's description of the Battle of Bunker Hill can be found in Henry Steele Commager and Richard B. Morris, eds., *The Spirit of 'Seventy-Six: The Story of the American Revolution as Told By Participants* (New York: Harper & Row, 1967), 132.

## Chapter 2

1  Nicholas Cresswell, *The Journal of Nicholas Cresswell, 1774–1777* (New York: The Dial Press, 1924), 179.

2  Quote from "The Testimony of Asher Wright," see George Dudley Seymour, *Documentary Life of Nathan Hale* (New Haven, CT: The Tuttle, Morehouse & Taylor Company, 1941), 316.

3  Full quote from "General Hull's Account of the Last Hours and Last Words of Hale," see Seymour, *Documentary Life of Nathan Hale*, 310; Hale's quote is referenced in Hannah Adams, *A Summary History of New-England* (Dedham, MA: H. Mann and J. H. Adams, 1799), 359.

4  An excerpt from Mackenzie's diary is included in Seymour, *Documentary Life of Nathan Hale*, 292.

5  George Washington, "General Orders," November 1, 1776, *Founders Online*, National Archives, https://founders.archives.gov/documents/Washington/03-07-02-0048.

6  George Washington to John Hancock, September 18, 1776, *Founders Online*, National Archives, https://founders.archives.gov/documents/Washington/03-06-02-0264.

7  This quote by Johannes Reuber is from an excerpt of his journal included in Bruce E. Burgoyne, ed., *Enemy Views: The American Revolutionary War as Recorded by the Hessian Participants* (Bowie, MD: Heritage Books, 1996), 104–105.

8  Quote included in Ron Chernow, *Alexander Hamilton* (New York: Penguin Books, 2004), 84.

9  George Washington to Samuel Washington, December 18, 1776, *Founders Online*, National Archives, https://founders.archives.gov/documents/Washington/03-07-02-0299.

10  This quote by Philipp Steuernagel is from an excerpt of his diary included in Bruce E. Burgoyne, ed., *Enemy Views*, 53.

11  George Washington to Samuel Washington, December 18, 1776, *Founders Online*, National Archives, https://founders.archives.gov/documents/Washington/03-07-02-0299.

12  John Greenwood, *The Revolutionary Services of John Greenwood of Boston and New York 1775–1783*, ed. Isaac J. Greenwood (New York: The De Vinne Press, 1922), 43.

13  This quote by Johannes Reuber is from an excerpt of his journal included in Bruce E. Burgoyne, ed., *Enemy Views*, 114.

14  This quote by Johannes Reuber is from an excerpt of his journal included in Bruce E. Burgoyne, ed., *Enemy Views*, 114–115.

15  This quote by Charles Willson Peale is from his diary and is included in Robert Middlekauff, *The Glorious Cause: The American Revolution, 1763–1789* (New York: Oxford University Press, 2007), 503.

16  This quote by David Harris, a veteran of the Battle of Princeton, is included in James Wilkinson, *Memoirs of My Own Times*, Vol. 1 (Philadelphia, PA: Albert Small, 1816), 145.

## Chapter 3

1  Baldwin is quoted in Richard M. Ketchum, *Saratoga: Turning Point of America's Revolutionary War* (New York: Henry Holt and Company, 1997), 436.

2  This quote by William Jolliffe is included in *The Parliamentary Register; or History of the Proceedings and Debates of the House of Commons*, Vol. 9 (London: J. Almon, 1778), 75.

3  This quote by Jäger officer Lieutenant Colonel Karl Adolf Christoph von Creuzbourg is included in Eric Schnitzer and Don Troiani, *Don Troiani's Campaign to Saratoga—1777: The Turning Point of the Revolutionary War in Paintings Artifacts, and Historical Narrative* (Guilford, CT: Stackpole Books, 2019), 101.

4  The National Archives (UK), WO27/35, "General Review of the 62nd Regiment of Foot," May 25, 1775.

5  James M. Hadden, *Hadden's Journal and Orderly Books: A Journal Kept in Canada and Upon Burgoyne's Campaign in 1776 and 1777*, ed. Horatio Rogers (Albany, NY: Joel Munsell's Sons, 1884), 164.

6  Benedict Arnold to George Washington, July 27, 1777, *Founders Online*, National Archives, https://founders.archives.gov/documents/Washington/03-10-02-0427.

7  George Washington, "General Orders," June 1, 1777, *Founders Online*, National Archives, https://founders.archives.gov/documents/Washington/03-09-02-0571.

8  Quote from Burgoyne's "Thoughts for conducting the War from the Side of Canada," February 28, 1777, included in John Burgoyne, *A State of the Expedition from Canada as Laid Before the House of Commons* (London: J. Almon, 1780), ix.

9  This quote by Henry Dundas is included in *The Parliamentary Register*, Vol. 8, 166, and Vol. 9, 78.

10  This quote is from the diary of Lieutenant William Heth, who was held as a prisoner in Quebec, quoted in Don Troiani and James L. Kochan, *Insignia of Independence: Military Buttons, Accoutrement Plates & Gorgets of the American Revolution* (Gettysburg, PA: Thomas Publications, 2012), 167.

## Chapter 4

1   Joseph Plumb Martin, *A Narrative of Some of the Adventures, Dangers, and Sufferings of a Revolutionary Soldier* (Hallowell, ME: Glazier, Masters & Co., 1830), 89

2   Martin, *A Narrative of Some of the Adventures, Dangers, and Sufferings of a Revolutionary Soldier*, 90

3   Martin, *A Narrative of Some of the Adventures, Dangers, and Sufferings of a Revolutionary Soldier*, 93.

4   Martin, *A Narrative of Some of the Adventures, Dangers, and Sufferings of a Revolutionary Soldier*, 93.

5   Martin, *A Narrative of Some of the Adventures, Dangers, and Sufferings of a Revolutionary Soldier*, 96-97.

6   John Romeyn Brodhead, ed., *Documents Relative to the Colonial History of the State of New York; Procured in Holland, England and France*, Vol. 8 (Albany, NY: Weed, Parsons and Company, 1857), 626.

7   Johann Ewald, *Treatise on Partisan Warfare*, trans. Robert A. Selig and David Curtis Skaggs (New York: Greenwood Press, 1991), 119.

8   Ewald, *Treatise on Partisan Warfare*, 119.

9   Charles Scott to George Washington, August 31, 1778, *Founders Online*, National Archives, https://founders.archives.gov/documents/Washington/03-16-02-0491.

10  John Graves Simcoe, *A History of the Operations of a Partisan Corps Called the Queen's Rangers* (New York: Bartlett & Welford, 1844), 85.

11  Johann Ewald, *Diary of the American War: A Hessian Journal*, trans. Joseph B. Tustin (New Haven, CT: Yale University Press, 1979), 145.

12  Ewald, *Diary of the American War*, 145.

13  This quote is from a report by Colonel Ichabod Alden to Brigadier General John Stark dated August 12, 1778, included in *Public Papers of George Clinton*, Vol. 5 (Albany, NY: James B. Lyon, 1901), 416.

14  This quote is from a letter by Captain Caldwell to Major John Butler dated September 21, 1778, included in M. Agnes Burton, ed., *Historical Collections: Collections and Researches made by the Michigan Pioneer and Historical Society*, Vol. 19 (Lansing, MI: Wynkoop Happenbeck Crawford Co., 1911), 356.

15  Martin, *A Narrative of Some of the Adventures, Dangers, and Sufferings of a Revolutionary Soldier*, 98–99.

16  Martin, *A Narrative of Some of the Adventures, Dangers, and Sufferings of a Revolutionary Soldier*, 99.

17  Ewald, *Diary of the American War*, 150.

18  Martin, *A Narrative of Some of the Adventures, Dangers, and Sufferings of a Revolutionary Soldier*, 99–100.

19  Ewald, *Diary of the American War*, 150.

20  Ewald, *Diary of the American War*, 151.

21  "Letters and Reports from Capt. Pausch, Hesse-Hanau Artillery, 1776–83," June 6, 1781, Tom. VII, Lidgerwood Collection of Hessian Transcripts, Morristown National Historical Park.

## Chapter 5

1   "Instructions to Major Ferguson, Inspector of Militia," May 22, 1780, Henry Clinton Papers, William L. Clements Library, The University of Michigan.

2   Ferguson is quoted in Stanley D. M. Carpenter, *Southern Gambit: Cornwallis and the British March to Yorktown* (Norman, OK: University of Oklahoma Press, 2009), 125.

3   Ferguson is quoted in Carpenter, *Southern Gambit*, 125.

4   Quote from "A statement of proceedings of the Western Army, from the 25th day of September, 1780, to the reduction of Major Ferguson and the army under his command" included in John H. Wheeler, *Historical Sketches of North Carolina from 1584 to 1851*, Vol. 1 (Philadelphia, PA: Lippincott, Grambo and Co., 1851), 104.

5   Quoted in Matthew H. Spring, *With Zeal and With Bayonets Only: The British Army on Campaign in North America, 1775–1783* (Norman, OK: University of Oklahoma Press, 2008), 257.

6   Quoted in Spring, *With Zeal and with Bayonets Only*, 257–258.

7   William Heath to George Washington, June 7, 1777, *Founders Online*, National Archives, https://founders.archives.gov/documents/Washington/03-09-02-0631.

8   Jeremiah Greenman, *Diary of a Common Soldier in the American Revolution, 1775–1783: An Annotated Edition of the Military Journal of Jeremiah Greenman*, Robert C. Bray and Paul E. Bushnell, eds., (DeKalb, IL: Northern Illinois University Press, 1978), 73.

9   This quote is from a letter by St. George Tucker and is included in Lawrence E. Babits and Joshua B. Howard, *Long Obstinate, and Bloody: The Battle of Guilford Courthouse* (University of North Carolina Press, 2009), 119.

## Chapter 6

1   James Forten to William Lloyd Garrison, February 23, 1831, Rare Books Department, Boston Public Library.

2   James Thacher, *A Military Journal During the American Revolutionary War, From 1775 to 1783* (Boston, MA: Cottons & Barnard, 1827), 263–264.

3   Quote from Rhode Island's 1778 "Act to Enlist Slaves," included in Judith L. Van Buskirk, *Standing in Their Own Light: African American Patriots in the American Revolution* (Norman, OK: University of Oklahoma Press, 2017), 102.

4    James Forten to William Lloyd Garrison, February 23, 1831, Rare Books Department, Boston Public Library.

5    James Forten to William Lloyd Garrison, February 23, 1831, Rare Books Department, Boston Public Library.

6    Armand Louis de Gontaut, *Memoirs of the Duc de Lauzun*, trans. E. Jules Méras (New York: Sturgis & Walton Company, 1912), 327.

7    George Washington, Diary Entry, September 30, 1781, *Founders Online*, National Archives, https://founders.archives.gov/documents/Washington/01-03-02-0007-0005-0009.

8    Quote from "Itinerary of the Pennsylvania Line from Pennsylvania to South Carolina, 1781–1782," *The Pennsylvania Magazine of History and Biography* 36, no. 3 (1912): 284.

9    Thacher, *A Military Journal During the American Revolutionary War, From 1775 to 1783*, 274.

10   Thacher, *A Military Journal During the American Revolutionary War, From 1775 to 1783*, 274.

11   George Washington, Diary Entry, October 9, 1781, *Founders Online*, National Archives, https://founders.archives.gov/documents/Washington/01-03-02-0007-0006-0003

12   Thacher, *A Military Journal During the American Revolutionary War, From 1775 to 1783*, 275.

13   Quote from "Diary of Events in the Army, From Aug. 1, 1780, to Dec. 31, 1780" included in John B. Linn and William H. Egle, eds., *Pennsylvania Archives, Second Series*, Vol. 11 (Harrisburg, PA: Lane S. Hart, 1880), 574.

14   Elias Dayton to Elias Dayton, October 19, 1781, transcribed by Howard C. Rice Jr., in "New & Notable," *The Princeton University Library Chronicle* 31, no. 3 (Spring 1970): 213.

15   A transcription of the Yorktown "Articles of Capitulation" is included in Jared Sparks, ed. *The Writings of George Washington*, Vol. 8, Part 2 (New York: Harper & Brothers Publishers, 1847), 533.

16   Ebenezer Denny, *Military Journal of Major Ebenezer Denny* (Philadelphia, PA: J. B. Lippincott & Co., 1859), 44; The "mortification and unfeigned sorrow" and "will never fade from my memory" statements are by British Captain-Lieutenant Samuel Graham, included in Max Hastings, ed., *The Oxford Book of Military Anecdotes* (New York: Oxford University Press, 1985), 175.

17   *The Pennsylvania Packet* (Philadelphia, PA), November 13, 1781.

18   Martin, *A Narrative of Some of the Adventures, Dangers, and Sufferings of a Revolutionary Soldier*, 168.

19   George Washington to Robert Hanson Harrison, November 18, 1781, *Founders Online*, National Archives, https://founders.archives.gov/documents/Washington/99-01-02-07418.

20   Anthony Wayne to Robert Morris, October 26, 1781, see Charles J. Stille, *Major-General Anthony Wayne and the Pennsylvania Line in the Continental Army* (Philadelphia, PA: J. B. Lippincott Company, 1893), 283.

21   Martin, *A Narrative of Some of the Adventures, Dangers, and Sufferings of a Revolutionary Soldier*, 205.

22   Martin, *A Narrative of Some of the Adventures, Dangers, and Sufferings of a Revolutionary Soldier*, 211–212.

23   Martin, *A Narrative of Some of the Adventures, Dangers, and Sufferings of a Revolutionary Soldier*, 202.

24   "An Act to provide for certain persons engaged in the land and naval service of the United States, in the Revolutionary War," March 18, 1818, *Acts of the Fifteenth Congress of the United States*, 410.

25   Joseph P. Martin, Revolutionary War Pension File, National Archives, M805, W1629, 11.

26   John P. Resch, "Politics and Public Culture: The Revolutionary War Pension Act of 1818," *Journal of the Early Republic* 8, no. 2 (Summer 1988): 155.

27   *Niles' Weekly Register* quoted in Resch, "Politics and Public Culture: The Revolutionary War Pension Act of 1818," 152.

28   Martin, *A Narrative of Some of the Adventures, Dangers, and Sufferings of a Revolutionary Soldier*, 212.

# ACKNOWLEDGMENTS

FOR THEIR GENEROUS ASSISTANCE, I AM PARTICULARLY GRATEFUL TO James L. Kochan, who shared his vast knowledge of eighteenth-century military uniforms and practically everything else throughout these projects, and to Dr. Coyle Connolly, collector and connoisseur of fine art. I also owe thanks to Lawrence E. Babits, Dan Blanchett, Joel R. Bohy, Todd W. Braisted, Matthew Brenckle, Christopher Bryant, Johnny F. Carawan, Rene Chartrand, Henry Cooke, David Dalrymple, Karie Diethorn, Robin Feret, Michael Flanagan, Erik Goldstein, Ray Halbritter, Ken Hamilton, Brian and Barbara Hendelson, Bruce Herman, Jim Hollister, Jerry Hurwitz, David J. Jackowe, Allan Jones, Matt Keagle, Doug Levering, Stuart Lilie, Bob McDonald, Joseph Malit, ZeeAnn Mason, Philip C. Mead, Kathryn Babbs Miller, Michelle Moskal, Colonel J. Craig Nannos, Cael O'Brian, Kian O'Brian, Ericka Osen, Ken Osen, Joe Painter, Shaun Pekar, Rebecca B. Phipps, Daniel M. Popek, Debbie Rebuck, John U. Rees, Steve Rogers, Bill Rose, George Savino, Judith Schnell, Eric Schnitzer, Robert A. Selig, Joseph Seymour, Matthew Skic, R. Scott Stephenson, Gregory Theberge, Jack Thomas Tomarchio, Anthony Wayne Tommell, David and Christa Troiani, Marc Troiani, Mark A. Turdo, Richard and Diane Ulbrich, Noel Walker, Schuyler C. Wickes, Ben R. Wolf, and all the great models who posed for me.

In addition to the Museum of the American Revolution, the following groups and institutions deserve my thanks: the Colonial Williamsburg Foundation, the Dietrich American Foundation, Independence National Historical Park, Minute Man National Historical Park, Museum of the First Troop of Philadelphia City Cavalry, the National Archives and Records Administration, the National Park Service, the Oneida Indian Nation, the Pennsylvania Society of Sons of the Revolution and its Color Guard, Saratoga National Historical Park, and the Washington-Rochambeau Revolutionary Route National Historic Trail.

Don Troiani
Southbury, Connecticut

The museum plaza at the corner of Third Street and Chestnut Street in Philadelphia

*Museum of the American Revolution*

# ABOUT THE MUSEUM OF THE AMERICAN REVOLUTION

IN 1903, DURING A SERMON COMMEMORATING GEORGE WASHINGTON'S birthday, Reverend W. Herbert Burk of All Saints' Episcopal Church in Norristown, Pennsylvania, announced an ambitious plan to construct a memorial to Washington at Valley Forge. While the Washington Memorial Chapel was being built, Burk also began acquiring artifacts as part of a dream to create a national museum dedicated to America's founding. In 1907, he launched a two-year fundraising effort to acquire Washington's original Revolutionary War tent. Burk opened a small museum within the chapel in 1909. In 1918, he established the Valley Forge Historical Society.

In 2003, the Museum of the American Revolution was created and inherited the Valley Forge Historical Society's collections. These efforts culminated in a historic land exchange with the National Park Service in 2010, when the Museum acquired the site of the former Independence National Historical Park Visitor Center in exchange for seventy-eight acres of privately owned land in Valley Forge. The Park Service was eager to acquire the parcel, which was adjacent to Valley Forge National Historical Park—and the Museum was thrilled to secure an ideal location in the heart of Philadelphia's historic district.

**Washington's War Tent**

*Museum of the American Revolution*

**The Museum of the American Revolution's core exhibit**
*Bluecadet*

The Museum began a $150 million campaign in 2010 to endow, build, and open the Museum of the American Revolution. During the demolition and construction process, the Museum was sensitive to the site's history, initiating an archaeological excavation. Archaeologists found eighty-five thousand artifact pieces, most of them from brick-lined privy and well shafts that were sealed beneath a later generation of buildings removed from the site.

Thanks to the generosity of H. F. (Gerry) and Marguerite Lenfest, along with private individuals from all fifty states, the Commonwealth of Pennsylvania, the Oneida Indian Nation, and foundations and corporate support, the Museum of the American Revolution opened to the public on April 19, 2017. Today, the Museum houses a rich collection of Revolutionary-era weapons, personal items, letters, diaries, and works of art.

It also includes immersive galleries, theater experiences, and recreated historical environments. These elements bring the events, people, and ideals of the nation's founding to life and engage people in the history and continuing relevance of the American Revolution. With a vision to ensure that the promise of the American Revolution endures, it is the Museum's mission to uncover and share compelling stories about the diverse people and complex events that sparked America's ongoing experiment in liberty, equality, and self-government.

This book has been published to accompany the special exhibit *Liberty: Don Troiani's Paintings of the Revolutionary War,* held at the Museum of the American Revolution from October 16, 2021 to September 5, 2022.

For more information, visit www.amrevmuseum.org.

# ABOUT THE CONTRIBUTORS

**Lawrence E. Babits** earned his PhD at Brown University. He has extensive experience in military and maritime archaeology and has excavated on battlefields, fortifications, ships, and a World War II POW camp. Babits served three years in the U.S. Army, largely with B Company, 1st Battalion, 21st Infantry (Gimlets). He has been a reenactor since 1961, especially as a Revolutionary War and Civil War private soldier. His travels include Egypt, Afghanistan, Iran, and Europe and sailing aboard tall ships. He is currently researching smoothbore musketry accuracy and shooting Civil War weaponry competitively with the First Maryland Infantry of the North-South Skirmish Association. He lives in Greenville, North Carolina.

**Joel Bohy** is the Director of Historic Arms & Militaria for Bruneau & Co Auctioneers and an appraiser on PBS's *Antiques Roadshow* for Arms & Militaria. He is an active member of the American Society of Arms Collectors and an instructor and board member for Advanced Metal Detecting for the Archaeologist. His passion for material culture and the history of the start of the American Revolution has led him to write and lecture with the Society for Historical Archaeology, the Fields of Conflict archaeology conference, Colonial Williamsburg's Weapons of War conference, the Concord Museum, and Minuteman National Historical Park.

**David J. Jackowe** is a physician and writer who has published numerous essays about American history, art, and medicine. He lives in Hastings-on-Hudson, New York, where he worked to commemorate the Battle of Edgar's Lane.

**James L. Kochan** spent nearly two decades as a museum director and curator, principally with the U.S. Army Museum System and the National Park Service. Prior to forming his own historical consulting and antiques business in 1998, he was director of museum collections at Mount Vernon, where he organized the blockbuster traveling exhibition, George Washington Revealed: Treasures from Mount Vernon. He is the recipient of numerous honors and awards for his curatorial and historical work and is the author or coauthor of many articles and books, including *Don Troiani's Soldiers of the American Revolution*. He often serves as a consultant to museums and historic sites as well as with the film/media industry and is the founding president of The Mars & Neptune Trust, a nonprofit dedicated to the study and preservation of early American military material culture.

**Bob McDonald** has been a student, researcher, and collector of American militaria (1775–1865) since childhood. He currently focuses on common soldier life through manuscript transcriptions from period diaries and collects American long arms, accouterments, Continental Army buttons, and personal items. He is a cofounder of www.RevWar75.com, which he invites you to visit.

**Philip C. Mead** is Chief Historian and Curator of the Museum of the American Revolution in Philadelphia. He received his doctorate in history from Harvard University, where his dissertation, *Melancholy Landscapes: Writing Warfare in Revolutionary America*, explored the ways that Revolutionary soldiers created the nation by describing its wartime appearance in their diaries. With R. Scott Stephenson, he co-curated the Museum of the American Revolution's core exhibition, which opened to the public in 2017. Since then, he has directed the museum's collections and special exhibitions team and has contributed to several books and exhibitions on early America and the American Revolution, including *Among His Troops: Washington's War Tent in a Newly Discovered Watercolor* and *When Women Lost the Vote: A Revolutionary Story, 1776–1807*.

**Eric Schnitzer,** author of *Don Troiani's Campaign to Saratoga—1777*, has been an interpreter and historian at Saratoga National Historical Park for twenty-five years. He is recognized for his writing and research on the Northern Campaign of 1777, having published numerous articles, given lectures, and provided historical editing and consultation for most publications on the subject. Eric earned a degree in history and fine art from SUNY Albany and is founder of the re-created 62nd Regiment of Foot. He lives in the White Creek Historic District, New York, with his wife, Jenna.

**Robert A. Selig** is a historical consultant who received his PhD in history from the *Universität Würzburg* in Germany in 1988. He has published several books on the American War of Independence as well as a translation of *A Treatise on Partisan Warfare* by Johann von Ewald, writes regularly for American and German scholarly and popular history magazines, and has contributed essays to anthologies such as *The American Revolution: A World War*. He is a specialist on the role of French forces under the Comte de Rochambeau during the American War of Independence and serves as project historian to the National Park Service for the Washington-Rochambeau Revolutionary Route National Historic Trail Project and as historian for various American Battlefield Protection Program projects.

**Matthew Skic** earned his MA from the University of Delaware's Winterthur Program in American Material Culture in 2016. His public history experience has included interpretation and curatorial work at Washington Crossing State Park in New Jersey and the Smithsonian Institution's National Museum of American History. He joined the curatorial team at the Museum of the American Revolution in 2016 and currently serves as Curator of Exhibitions. Matthew is the author of the book *Cost of Revolution: The Life and Death of an Irish Soldier* (2019) and co-author, with R. Scott Stephenson, Philip C. Mead, and Mark A. Turdo, of *Among His Troops: Washington's War Tent in a Newly Discovered Watercolor* (2019). He lives in Moorestown, New Jersey.

**Gregory Theberge**, a Rhode Island native, can usually be found researching some aspect of American or British history when he's not practicing periodontics and implant dentistry.

Whether documenting eighteenth-century material culture, common soldier tents and kitchens used during the American Revolution, the brewing industry of his home state, or mid-twentieth-century Tiki establishments, he credits his father, Ed, for his love for history. Theberge has been involved with progressive living history organizations since 1977. His research on the Boston Massacre is extensive and he was honored to serve as historical advisor to Don Troiani for his painting of the event.

**Anthony Wayne Tommell** is a retired historian/interpreter and museum curator. He worked for a number of Historic Sites/Parks in the National Park Service system. He was also the Curator of Ordnance and Heavy Equipment for the U.S. Marine Corps Museum at Quantico, Virginia. He has worked with Don Troiani on several projects including the Wayside Exhibits for Saratoga National Historical Park. Anthony's most intense and detailed research centered on the Burgoyne Campaign of 1777. He was the principal coauthor of the foreword of John R. Elting's book, *The Battles of Saratoga*, published in 1977. Anthony continues to enjoy researching. He lives in upstate New York with his wife of many years.